To,

Ken

Pauline

Hope Beyond the Bruises

Pauline Ngure

authorHOUSE™

1663 LIBERTY DRIVE, SUITE 200
BLOOMINGTON, INDIANA 47403
(800) 839-8640
WWW.AUTHORHOUSE.COM

First published by AuthorHouse 10/19/05

ISBN: 1-4208-7948-0 (sc)

Printed in the United States of America
Bloomington, Indiana

This book is printed on acid-free paper.

Dedication

...to my sons Bryan and Kevin, who survived abuse from their father

...to women and children all over the world who suffer domestic abuse

...to victims and survivors of domestic violence

Table of Contents

Acknowledgements

A big thank you to my mom and dad, my brothers Ndaba and Tom, the Women's Rights Awareness Program, in Nairobi, particularly to Anne Ngugi.

I thank the Federation of Women Lawyers Kenya, especially Judy Thongori. These dedicated people and their organizations stood by us and suffered at the hands of the Kenya police and JB for a whole year. They never stopped supporting me, even when arrested and threatened by the police.

I thank Linnie for your support and prayers; they kept me going. Maria - you are like a sister; Susan - you are a great woman; Sarah – your one and only visit to us worked miracles for us. All the dedicated and supportive staff of UNHCR Kampala who did not rest until the last day; Amos—you are more than a brother, driving us to all those places even when it was risky.

I thank the Canadian High Commission in Nairobi and Kampala, and Citizenship and Immigration Canada for their great job and continuous support.

I thank my best friend Anita for always being available when I need someone to talk to.

Thank you Jared in Stockholm—you never stopped communicating with me, even when the going was tough.

Thank you Elaine my boss for all your support.

Thank you David my dedicated and great editor.

I appreciate the support from the Kenya print and electronic media for listening to me, for highlighting my story and that of other victims that they continue to highlight. Please do not give up the fight; someday the Kenya government may hear and do their duty. To you and many more individuals and organizations, no words can express my gratitude. Thank you *so* much.

. . . .

Kenyan Woman

Women in Kenya are vulnerable to poverty, HIV infection (which is believed to kill three people every five minutes), and violence because of discriminatory property inheritance practices. Poverty and traditionalism remain two major obstacles to women's equal rights in Kenya. The media favours women's rights, but the traditional law status is hard to overcome in Kenyan society. In some tribes, traditional culture allows a man to discipline his wife by physical means; there is no law that prohibits spousal rape. Women in Kenya are generally murdered, brutalized, and terrorized by their male partners every day while the government sits and watches because it is clear that women in Kenya are second-class citizens.

The problem of girl child rape and molestation is growing every day. According to Kenyan law, a man does not rape a girl who is under fourteen years. If he has sexual intercourse with such a girl against her will, he is charged with a lesser offence of child molestation that carries a very minimal jail sentence. Some male schoolteachers molest and rape children, especially in rural areas. A number of men who are infected with HIV AIDS have a silly belief that if they have sexual intercourse with a virgin, they will be cured. The many rapes of minor girls in Kenya leave the girls infected with the HIV virus.

Wife inheritance is one of the oldest and probably most barbaric practices among some tribes in Kenya.

When one's husband dies, a brother or a cousin of her late husband automatically takes in the woman as a wife. This is mostly practised in Nyanza province. This region has the highest number of HIV AIDS cases in the country. After one's husband dies, a woman is often evicted, made penniless, or forced to engage in demeaning and risky sexual practices and cleansing rituals—mostly with a man of a lower social standing, thus risking HIV infection to stay in her late husband's property. Women who refuse to be inherited face violence or even rape; those who escape often end up penniless, living in Nairobi's burgeoning slums. If a woman refuses to be inherited and continues to stay in her late husband's property, her late husband's relatives might drive her away from home and declare a curse on her and her children.

Ironically, when a wife dies, the man is free to marry whomever he pleases. There is no law that dictates men will be inherited by their brother's wives. They even inherit women who are as old as sixty-two. In most cases, some of these men's wives may have died of AIDS but they knowingly go ahead and infect other innocent women in the name of inheritance.

Inheritance laws, be they customary or legal, are biased against women, especially in relation to family land and other property. In rural areas, for example, customary practises result in patriarchal land being inherited by sons and not daughters. Legally, widows, for example, only have a life interest over their deceased husband's land property and/or estate. They lose the estate when they remarry. They cannot dispose or bequeath said land, property and/or estate. Widowers are not bound by the same rules; even where land, property and/or estate belonged to their deceased wives. Wife inheritance in some communities also disenfranchises women in that control of matrimonial property and, to some extent, control of their lives, is relinquished to their deceased husband's brothers or cousins.

Under customary laws of most ethnic groups, a woman cannot inherit land, and must live on the family land as a guest of male relatives by blood or marriage. Most titles to the land in Kenya are made out in the man's name—even if you buy property as a couple. Statistics indicate that women are the backbone of the country's agricultural sector. This means that many women produce food and develop the land with no legal or cultural rights to the same. Land, therefore, is not an economic asset for such women, since their access to land is tied up with their relationship to men. They cannot use land as a security in loan acquisition; at the same time they have difficulty moving into non-traditional fields. In the work place, women are promoted more slowly than men, and bear the brunt of layoffs.

Women continue to face legal and actual discrimination in many areas. A married woman cannot obtain a national identity card or a passport without her husband's consent. On the other hand, it does not matter whether a man is married or not because he automatically qualifies for a passport or the national identity card without his wife's consent.

Section 82 of the Kenyan Constitution does not protect women fully against discrimination. Discrimination against women is allowed under personal law. This means that in issues of inheritance, adoption, and devolution of property on death, a man's customs take precedence. The government and courts always choose the man's customs. If a Kenyan man marries a wife from outside Kenya, the lady automatically becomes a Kenyan citizen but if a Kenyan lady marries a foreigner neither her husband nor the children will ever be Kenyans.

Kenya does not have comprehensive legislation on the issue of matrimonial property. In the absence of such legislation, Kenyan courts have relied on The Married Women's Property Act of England—1882. However, it is mostly the appellate courts that refer to the Act, which means that many women cannot afford to get fair divorce judgements. The process involves costs of instigating the suit and of legal representation at the lower courts, and extra costs in the appellate courts. It is to be noted that, according to legal precedence, women rarely get favourable judgements in lower courts.

Institutionalised corruption and the lack of legislation governing ethics (code of conduct) of leaders result in weighted justice; that is, justice is dispensed according to the contents of one's wallet or according to who has a more influential political godfather. This makes the lives of women married to influential or affluent men difficult, especially in the face of spousal abuse, since husbands can use their social, economic, or political clout to ignore court orders such as those pertaining to child custody or restraining orders. Such men are in a position to influence police officers to harass and intimidate in-laws, non-governmental organisations, or any other persons or institutions to which their wives may have turned for help.

Discrimination against women is more apparent in rural areas. Most families who live in very remote areas are more reluctant to invest in educating girls than boys, especially at the higher level even if the girl is doing better in school than the boy. Education is very expensive in Kenya; that is why most parents prefer to invest in boys, not girls. More than seventy percent of the illiterate people in Kenya are women. In such cases, discrimination against women starts from home.

Women experience a wide range of discriminatory practices, limiting their political and economic rights and relegating them to second-class citizenship. Even those women who are elected to parliament are not able to talk for their fellow women because only three of thirty cabinet ministers are female. Any time they raise a motion in support of women, it is usually defeated because they are the minority. In 1993 the attorney general established a task force on laws relating to women. As of 2005, it has yet to make its report.

Forced marriage is another major problem affecting young girls. Some fathers marry off their daughters when they are as young as thirteen. Mostly, they are married off to rich old men who are not only old enough to be their fathers but also grandfathers. A father can comfortably marry off his thirteen-year-daughter to an old man who is sixty years old or more. In most cases such a girl would be a third or even a fourth wife. A thirteen year old is a minor according to the law but the government rarely intervenes. Since girls are treated like commodities; when a rich man shows up in a poor family's home where there are young girls and offers to buy one, it is to the pleasure of the family. Since he pays for the girl, he has complete rights over her. Both parties sign documents stating the terms and conditions and the amount paid as dowry.

Dowry, also known as bride price, makes men feel they have bought a woman and so they feel they have all rights to treat her as personal property. Even if one is not marrying off a daughter, dowry is widely practiced traditionally among many tribes in Kenya. The man's family goes to the girl's home and both parties bargain on how much the man's family will pay for the dowry. If the man is not able to pay the whole amount at once, he is allowed to pay in instalments (in North America it would be payment plan) until payment is made in full. This gives the husband power to control and to treat his wife as his personal property since he bought her. During these negotiations, the girl's relatives, especially women, show up and demand payment of any damage the girl may have caused when young. For example, if she broke a calabash or a cooking pot, the man could be forced to pay as much as ten times the value of a pot.

Certain ethnic groups practise female genital mutilation, despite being widely condemned internationally as physically and psychologically damaging. It is widespread, particularly in rural areas. In addition to depriving women of sexual pleasure, the practice often has serious health implications such as infections, cystitis, sterility, birth complications, and, in many documented cases, death. Tribes that practice this primitive and barbaric act believe that for a woman to be well behaved, she must be mutilated. Women's rights organizations have been trying—without success—to persuade the government to prohibit female genital mutilation.

Street children face harassment, especially girls. They are physically and sexually abused by the police and within the juvenile justice system. They are arrested and held in extremely harsh conditions in crowded police station cells, often without toilets (they use buckets as toilets) or bedding, with little or no food. They are mixed with adults and frequently raped or beaten up by the police.

Domestic violence in Kenya, which defies any statistical measure, hinges on the fear factor. The message from Kenyan men who violate women rights is domination. Women must stay in their place or be afraid. Because this is the case, most Kenyan women *are* afraid. If your husband is a wife barterer, it means you are sitting up in the night, waiting for him to return from his rendezvous with fellow drinkers. You dare not go to bed before he comes home. That alone warrants a thorough beating. You do not have any right to ask why he is late or where he has been.

Domestic violence, rape, incest, girl child defilement even when they are as young as three years old, forced marriage, abuse of housemaids, and the arrest and torture of women by police to lure male suspects to come out of hiding are the order of the day in Kenya. A woman being locked up in police cells on their rich husband's orders is common practice. Police go to the extent of bottle raping women and pulling out their hair to get the information or to force them to sign doctored statements.

Robbery with violence in Kenya, be it car jacking or burglary, is accompanied by rape. They rape daughters and their mothers—no matter what age. The violence is malicious and brutal. It is calculated to be humiliating—almost like a vendetta. According to the latest statistics, two women are raped hourly in Kenya and the figures are going up. This trend is attributed to laxity in prosecuting the crime and the high percentage of acquittals on flimsy grounds. Currently, women's rights organizations in Kenya are campaigning for a law that would see men castrated as a consequence of being convicted of rape. This probably would scare would-be rapists; they will think twice before committing the offence. But since men are the lawmakers, it will be very difficult for such a law to be passed. This is not about women and what they have done and not done. It is about men, power, and control. What they are saying to their targets is that they can do anything and get away with it. Reason: they are men and the law protects men and cares less about women. People who care and think positively about women and children should join the fight against male violence. Women continue to suffer because they are women, as if it is a crime to be a woman.

In the police station, the victim of domestic violence rarely gets an officer empathetic to her suffering. All she gets is ridicule, being taunted that she's unable to keep her man happy or that she is unable to keep a home. Many officers advise women in such predicaments to go home and make up with their husbands and learn to love them. This occurs even when there is proof of aggravated assault, battery, death threats, and other criminal actions. Some women opt to go to elders for arbitration of marital disputes.

However, such elders only involve themselves in matters pertaining to dowry upon the dissolution of a marriage. The affected women rarely get any redress for their suffering. The elders fear that if they agree to dissolve the marriage, the man will demand back the dowry, which they cannot afford to pay, so the woman continues to suffer because the man paid money to buy them.

I lived in Uganda for one year in 2002. I was shocked to read in the newspapers that Uganda's vice-president, a woman, was being battered by her husband. "I am a reference book to other Ugandan women," she said. "Everyone thought my life was perfect. I had a husband, a career, and money; my children were doing well in school and university, and yet I was miserable in my marriage because of the abuse. I finally had enough of living the life people expected me to lead and decided to break my silence about what was really going on. My hope is that others will find the courage to say no to violence that is in so many of our homes but is rarely spoken about."

When the vice president's husband was interviewed he admitted having hit her "once or twice." If a woman in such a senior position cannot get help from the police, what about Njeri, Jane, Lucy and others?

Some men in Africa think by hurting women they are more manly than others. They have the mentality that if a woman is holding a more senior position at work than them, they have to prove they are still the head by hitting them.

Kenyan police use their work to intimidate and rape women. They continue to do that while in full uniform. If a woman is raped by a police officer, where does she go to report? Some of the things that Kenyan police forces do are shocking.

The following story was carried in one of the leading newspapers in Kenya. The media does a great job in highlighting women's plight but it takes only a short time for Kenyans to be shocked about terrible crimes against humanity, raise their voices in anger and condemnation, and then get back to their lives. The crime forgotten; there is no follow up because justice in Kenya, especially where women and the poor are concerned, does not exist.

Saturday January 8, 2005

Raped for failing to raise Shillings 5,000 bribe

A police officer accused of raping a woman who failed to bribe him is on the run.

The officer, attached to Nairobi's Pangani police station, is said to have forcibly had sex with the woman on Friday night after she failed to part with Sh5,000.

Narrating her ordeal, the married woman said the officers stormed into their hotel room on Friday evening and demanded the bribe to spare her arrest for not carrying along her identity card.

The woman, who sought help at the Standard offices, said her husband tried in vain to raise the money from more than five shops at the Garissa Lodge trading mall.

While he was away, however, the officers allegedly drove off with the 24-year-old woman to Pangani police station.

The two officers then commandeered her into a bar opposite the station, where they reportedly drank four beers each.

"I watched them drink and then one of them said he was returning me to the hotel to see if my husband had come back," said the woman.

Outside the bar, she was allegedly handcuffed and ordered to walk to a nearby lodging where the officer had booked a room.

A receptionist at the lodging said the man demanded to be booked into a room with a mosquito net. "It is true she came here in the company of a man who booked a room."

Inside the room, she pleaded with the policeman not to rape her, but he allegedly tied her legs to the bed using bed-sheets, and then gagged her with a towel.

The woman said she lost consciousness and when she woke up in the morning, the man gave her Sh100 for fare and advised her to raise Sh5,000 by midday.

In normal circumstances things like these do not happen. They happen only in novels and in action movies and of course in real life in Kenya. Kenya is one of the African countries that prides itself as being democratic. A person like me, who was born and raised there, knows it is one of the most unequal societies in the world. But if you want to go and see the wildlife and enjoy the sunshine at the Indian Ocean beaches, it is great.

When my husband (a person I will refer to in this narrative as JB because he is and was never worthy to be my husband) became a real threat to my life and to that of my two sons, we ran for our lives across the boarder to the Ugandan capital of Kampala in January 2002. Six months later nothing was happening. My parents and brothers and some women's rights organizations in Kenya had tried in vain to get government protection for us. One morning in June 2002, I woke up frustrated, with a bad feeling of hopelessness. I had cried and prayed the whole night. I had a terrible headache and my eyes were swollen. My elder son Bryan could understand, as he was six years old then. My small one was just one year. Bryan asked me, "Mom are you ok?" I screamed "NOOOO!" and cried loudly. Bryan hugged me and told me "Mom, don't worry. God is with us. We shall one day get out of here and we shall be free. Mom, I love you and I thank you for removing us from where we were being beaten and abused."

From that day, I got new strength and courage. I promised not to let my children down; I was not going to give up the fight no matter how difficult it was going to be. I had no idea where we would go or what I was going to do but I was determined not to give up the fight against JB. In the same way he had declared war on me, vowing not to give up until he got hold of me. To keep sane, I decided to do something because I was sitting the whole day without doing anything apart from the small household chores as we lived in a very small house. Later that day, I went to the nearest shop, bought a writing pad and a pen and started to write about my life and that of my children in an abusive home.

You will see in my story how I lived with a man in the name of a husband for ten years. He was a combination of a male chauvinist, molester, child abuser, wife batterer, sadist, terrorist, and a person who suffered from inferiority complex. This is a person who would tell lies, without caring what happens when the truth came out. He believed in bribery, corruption, and the power of money. He used to ask people if they would prefer to be bribed or to support me and suffer. He was a person who bought justice with money; he bought my brother so he could swear an affidavit against me. He had no respect for anybody, even for his parents. He believed he had the capability of breaking the law, and since he had money, he could buy anybody at any time, including justice.

He hurt my children and me physically, mentally, and psychologically for ten years. He hurt my father when I sought refugee in my parents' house. He would tear off my clothes, whip me naked, rape me, and force me to my knees to apologize and promise I would never leave him and that I loved him. He could beat the kids senseless. I could not protect them; if I tried, I paid dearly. Whenever I ran away from him, he would get me back by force, threaten to kill me, and sometimes use the police to have me locked in police cells until I agreed to go back to live with him. I had to bribe some criminals with whom I was locked up in the police cells so that they would not rape me. Being locked up in the police cells with rapists, robbers, murderers, druggist, and all types of criminals on my husband's orders was one of the worst experiences I went through during my married life. I remember one woman who seemed to have lived in that cell for the longest and who behaved like a head girl. She asked why I was there. That is a very common question when you get into the police cells in Kenya. I told her my husband took me there. Her advice? "Kill him!" She said she could give me contacts of people who could do it in hours for just a couple thousand shillings.

He "loved" me so much that he could beat me until I lost conscious, to the extent of getting a miscarriage. He pulled out my hair, locked my son in the house without food or water, and refused to allow him to go to school. I had nobody to turn to. When the neighbours reported him to the children's department, he bribed the magistrate and was let go. The Kenyan police ridiculed me, beat me up, and called me names because I had run away from an abusive husband.

My Background

I am the last born in a family of eight, four boys and four girls. Born in Limuru (one of the coldest areas in Kenya – but not comparable to Canada), Kiambu district, Central Province. I never lived with my eldest sister as a sister at home, because when I was born she was already married. At one time I could not believe she was my sister; I thought she was an aunt, but as I grew up, I realized she was my sister, as my brothers and sisters called her by name but not aunt.

My father was working as a manager in a tea plantation, one of the largest tea estates in Kenya. He said he had worked there ever since he was a young man. He used to wake as early as 4 a.m., made his breakfast, being careful not to make any noise lest he woke us. After that he would wake Mom up to lock the door as he left quietly for work. We would not see him until late in the evening. He was a kind, loving father and as far as I can remember, he never raised a finger or called my mom names. If we did anything wrong, he would call us and talk to us and ask us not to repeat the mistake. I never experienced violence or name calling in my home and when my husband started hurting and calling me names, it was something new to me. How I managed for ten years under my husband's tyranny remains a mystery.

We did not have a lot of money but we had clothes and enough to eat; my parents were able to send each of us to school. School fees in Kenya are expensive so it was a big sacrifice for them to educate all of us. In those days, most parents could only pay school fees for the boys; girls were to stay home, grow up, and get married. My parents knew the value of education and treated all of us equally by giving us the best education of the time.

My mother was kind-hearted, hard working, and more talkative than my father. She would work on the farm while we were in school. She did all the household work and cooked for us. In the evening, we shared chores. My two elder sisters would help in cooking, while my two elder brothers fed and milked the cows and made sure the sheds were locked. Since I was the youngest and considered a baby, I did light chores, after which my brothers helped me with my homework. While we sat around the fireplace waiting for dinner, Mother would sometimes read interesting stories by Kenyan author Fred K. Kago. Dinner in Kenya is served between 8 and 9 p.m.

I finished elementary education and proceeded to high school. I remember vividly when I went to form one (grade nine in North America) one of my brothers, who was already working, escorted me to boarding school. He advised me to work hard and not to agree to be cheated by boys. He told me there was nothing they could offer me apart from lying to me, and disrupting my education, making my future miserable because without a good education, one cannot get a good job. I promised my brother he could count on me to be a good girl and to work hard. I kept my word. I was lucky to have such a brother because according to our Kikuyu tradition, a brother is not supposed to discuss such issues with his sister. I worked hard in school, did well in my final examination, and joined a secretarial college in Nairobi, Kenya's capital city.

After college I found a job as a secretary in a law firm and was doing well financially. I was the envy of everybody from my village and a good example to girls still in school. Most parents used to tell their daughters, "I want you to study as hard as Njeri and become a secretary like her." Being a secretary and working in the biggest city in Kenya and working in one of the most reputable law firms was something important. Some of them thought I was a lawyer! My parents were proud of me, as most of my friends after high school either got pregnant or married without going to college, university, or getting a job. I was one girl who, when the neighbours heard I was home for the weekend, would flock into our homestead to greet me.

Marriage – I would never hurt a fly

Daily Nation November 25 2004

No more of this Violence, please!
By Lucy Oriang' (Managing Editor)

I first met the young woman in Entebbe, Uganda. She was Kenyan, like myself, and we might as well have met in Nairobi. But she was a woman on the run, though not in the traditional sense. Being on the run is for criminals fleeing justice, but Njeri was desperate to escape her husband and the father of her two sons.

As I arrived at the swanky hotel she was staying in, I saw a woman no more than 33 hanging around the reception, trying desperately to fit in. But I knew instinctively that she was the person I had an assignment with. My journey had been a pretty clandestine affair; full of the kind of intrigue I had previously seen only in movies. It was not until I arrived at the Jomo Kenyatta International Airport that I learnt my destination. Having arrived, I could feel her vetting me from a distance before she dropped her guard and approached.

Our lives would touch ever so fleetingly—three hours in all—but Njeri would remain in my mind and in my heart for two years. Whenever I think of Njeri now, the first word that comes to my mind is fear—in capital letters. Njeri spoke of her estranged husband with the kind of terror that should not belong in a marriage.

Her first born, old enough to know what was going on around him, was far too grown-up for a child aged only six, so fiercely protective of his mother that he refused to go more than two meters away when bidden to go play by the pool side. In the end, we let him be. After all, the assaults we would speak of were nothing new; he had been witness to it all.

Formally married

Njeri's agony began long ago. He first beat her because she came home late from work, and this was a time they were not even formally married. He would go on to beat her right in her parents' homestead and in the presence of his own parents and siblings. It is unheard of in most African communities for anyone to beat a woman in her own parents' house and subject the in-laws to public humiliation and threats. But such was his towering rage that none of his own relatives ever thought to intervene.

Not even her flight in 2002 to the battered women's shelter in Nairobi run by the Women's Rights Awareness Program could save her from the distress. He was always one step ahead, arriving in person to bully the staff, threatening everyone through cell phone, letters, and email. As we spoke, Njeri constantly looked over her shoulders because, she confided, he had even managed to track her to the home of a local women's rights activist and threatened her with what we Kenyans call "dire consequences."

I returned home subdued, only for the news to break a couple of days later. The man, curiously enough a senior officer in an international non-governmental organization, was threatening to sue anyone who carried the story. Njeri's parents were on air and everywhere they thought they could get help for their daughter.

Exposing the violence

I remember her mother, looking me in the eye and begging me to help find ways of exposing the violence that her youngest daughter had been subjected to for so long. Her brothers spoke of intimidation by a man who seemed to have the resources to hire 24-hour surveillance of the family—just in case they could lead him to the woman who was now more his quarry than his wife.

Njeri now lives far away with her sons across the seas, having received asylum in a developed country. She is lucky in a sense: she can, at least, wipe clean the slate and start all over again. Why she had to run away from home in order to get a guarantee of security is the subject of You and I can make a commitment today 16 Days of Activism Against Gender Violence. *To begin the process of recognizing women's rights as human rights and End the Violence!*

Njeri is none other than me. You may have noticed that the interview with Lucy was in March 2002 and the story was carried in November 2004. That was how powerful JB was. So powerful that even the media houses feared him because whoever carried the story would have been a victim of his terrorism. Thanks be to God that his power of money is no longer there and that at least the media can use my story to educate other women who may be hanging in there in abusive relationships.

We all meet our future partners under different circumstances. When I first met my ex-husband, a man I said earlier that I will refer him as JB, on January 01, 1992, he was driving a commuter taxi that I had boarded with my brother Tom, to pay a visit to our parents in their upcountry home in Limuru. This area is just thirty-four kilometers from Nairobi.

When all the other passengers had alighted, my brother asked the driver to take us to my parents' home at an extra charge. When we arrived, my mother invited him to join us for lunch, because in our Kikuyu custom, one entering your home in a friendly way is offered food or something to drink. My brother requested that driver to come back and pick us up for our trip back to Nairobi. He accepted and on the way back was very inquisitive, asking me what I did and where I lived. I learnt that he worked as an auditor with one of the government ministries in Nairobi but said that driving taxis was a hobby. He was a very handsome man and we just hit it off. This was the kind of guy any girl would love to be seen with. We used to describe such guys as Tall, Dark, and Handsome (TDH). I would have been a fool to refuse his offer for lunch the following day.

Two months after we met, we started staying together. In Nairobi when a woman and a man start staying together without a wedding or the customary ceremonies, we call it *come we stay*. When he asked me to go stay with him, I did not hesitate. He was a good man and promised me that after a few months we should do a wedding. I had no reason to doubt him. When we started dating we were meeting for lunch on a daily basis and for evening coffee before each one went home. He was strong and protective. We always held hands when we walked. It doesn't happen quite often in Kenya.

My girlfriends and colleagues at work really liked him. He could drop me at work, come over at lunchtime so we could go for lunch. He would pick me up in the evening. I later realized that he was doing all that out of jealousy; he did not want me to have any friends or to talk with other people including my relatives. I was all his. When he realized I had lost all my friends, the "honey moon" ended and I became very lonely.

Since we met, I had not met any of his friends or relatives. When I asked him about his friends he would tell me that as long as I was with him, nobody else mattered. To me it seemed ok because he was always with me. What else would I have needed if my boyfriend was with me twenty-four hours a day? I was to learn later that he avoided his friends because he had another wife who had taken off with his kids. Probably he thought they would tell me.

On Friday evenings he would pick me up from work and we would go for coffee, then to the movies, then for dinner, and home. This was the kind of life we lived. Monday to Thursday we would go straight home after work. We used to have good conversations and jokes. He told me frequently how he loved me and that he would never leave me or do anything to hurt me. He asked me if I loved him as much as he loved me and if I would ever leave him. I told him if he became mean to me I would leave. He used to tell me that he could not hurt a fly and so there was no way he could be mean to me. I did not know that I was going to be his slave and that no matter how much he hurt me, I would never be able to leave him.

Things were going very well for us until April 1992 when one Friday my boss requested that I come in the next day to help with some urgent work. When we reached home that Friday evening, I told him I had been asked to work the following day. He did not say a word. On Saturday morning I asked him to give me a ride to work, but he refused without explanation. Since I had not seen him in that kind of a mood, I just went to work and left him sleeping. That was the day my problems started.

I worked until 4 p.m. He did not call me at the office as he usually did. There was no cause for alarm; I just thought he was tired and wanted to rest. When I went back home, I found him standing at the gate. Without uttering a word to me, he started beating me right there at the gate. It was near a path and people were passing by. Generally in Kenya, when a man is beating a woman, and people ask him why he is doing it, he answers that she is his wife. Even if he is killing you, they will not help you. In other words, when you are a married woman, you automatically are your husband's property and he can do what pleases him, even if it means killing you. If a man is beating you and he says you are a prostitute and that you have stolen his money, they will encourage him to beat you even more. I did not understand why he was beating me and for once I thought I was dreaming. I tried to run away but he was faster and stronger. He carried me into the house where he beat me even more. I though he was going to kill me. He removed my clothes and started checking me, telling me I had been sleeping with men. I pleaded with him, but he would not listen. I was in shock; I never thought at any time anybody could do such things to me—mostly my loving boyfriend. I kept asking myself why and how dare he beat me? That was the beginning of my problems and it was not going to stop until ten years later when I had to flee the country with my sons. The person whom I made a mistake of staying with made my children and I refugees.

After he was done beating me up, he carried me to bed and raped me repeatedly. I was bleeding from the wounds he had inflicted. At 10 p.m. he asked me to get up, put on my nice evening dress because he was going to take me out to dance! I was scared and pleaded that I was feeling sick and would not be able to dance. He slapped me across the face so hard that I went sprawling off the bed. I got the strength to dress; my face was swollen and had lots of pain. When I tried to talk to him to let me rest, he told me he would lay me on the ground, take a pair of pliers and pluck out my teeth one by one. That was the last thing I wanted to happen, so I got ready. At the club, he ordered meat and ugali (an African favorite food made of corn flour and water; it looks like mashed potatoes but is more white). I could not chew the meat because my jaws and teeth were hurting. He forced me to dance with him. When we went back home it was 5 a.m.; he raped me again and I knew in my heart that I would go to my parents and never return to him.

On Monday morning I went to work and asked for permission to leave because I still had pain in my body. I went back to the house, picked up my clothes, and fled to my parents' house. I told them what had happened and they asked me never to go back to him. The following morning when I went to work, I found him at the entrance of my office waiting for me. He apologized and promised me that he would *never* beat me again and that he did not know why he did that because he was a peaceful person. I refused to listen to him. In the evening I found him again waiting for me at the same place. He grabbed me and forced me in his car and drove me home at a very high speed without even saying a word to me. He was a strong person and he used to lift me up physically to the amusement of my colleagues and passers-by. I was so scared I knew my life had come to an end. When we reached home, he asked me to choose between staying with him and death. Of course I chose to stay with him. He threatened and promised to kill me if I ever attempted to leave him again. I got so scared that I kept on thinking one day he will get angry with me and kill me. From that day on he became very hostile—it was the beginning of real trouble.

He was a Kikuyu from Nyeri where history has it that women from there are very aggressive. Because of the mistreatment from their husbands, they beat them up. So most men from Nyeri (it is a district in the central province of Kenya) do not like to marry girls from their district. On the other hand, in Kiambu (another district in central Kenya and where I come from), men are generally polite and do not believe in wife beating even though there are still a few cases.

He was always mad with me but when he was with other people he was an angel. Beating me became the order of the day. He would beat me in the streets, in his office, in the car, in a restaurant, in friends' houses, in his parents' house, in my parents' house; even when I accidentally hit the gate to the entrance of our house with my car, he beat me up in front of our security guard.

He imposed a new rule: I had to leave my workplace at exactly 5 p.m. whether I had work to do or not. It was not his problem. I had to walk to his office and wait for him even if it meant up to 9 p.m. Sometimes he locked me in his office as early as 5:15 p.m. and leave me there. I don't know where he went and of course I had no right to ask. Any attempt to question or refuse ended in a beating. Even if we reached home at 10 p.m., that was when I would start to cook. I had to do the cleaning after dinner, and he would go to sleep, leaving me to do the housework. Sometimes I could go to bed as late as 1 a.m. He had another rule: I had to wake at 5 a.m. to warm his bathing water, make his breakfast, re-iron his shirt (because I used to iron them on weekends) then go and wake him up softly and slowly like a baby. I do not think even a servant would be subjected to such humiliation.

By that time, I was not supposed to visit my parents without him accompanying me, nor was I allowed to talk to my brothers or sisters. I had no permission to have friends and nobody was allowed to visit me. I was in total isolation.

One evening in June of 1992, he came home angry. He picked a fight by asking how many men call me at work. I told him no men called me at work. He insisted and told me that if I did not tell him, he would use force. I knew he was out to hurt me so I kept quiet. He started slapping and kicking me. I cried and pleaded for mercy but he would not stop. I decided to scream because I feared he would kill me. The landlord came to my rescue but he refused to open the door. After he was satisfied, he raped me. Without even showering, he asked me to dress up because he was taking me for a dance yet again. I had pain all over my body and told him I was feeling sick and could not go. He told me if I refused he would beat me again and this time he was going to make sure I was dead. When he was about to hurt me he could go mad with rage. He could foam at the mouth and shake. So I did as he said. We went to a club on airport road. He bought meat and drinks and asked me to eat lots because I was so thin that I was an embarrassment to him. He told me how much he loved me and the thought of losing me drove him crazy.

At the end of 1992, we moved into a bigger house. He imposed the rule of the pay check: on payday, I was supposed to give him my entire pay check. I could no longer buy anything or save because I had to beg money from him. Sometimes, he would give me a few shillings for lunch. When he telephoned my office and found I was not on my desk, he would beat me when we got home that evening. Sometimes I would be in my boss's office or in the washroom. He did not care. I was tired of telling my brothers and my parents. I was embarrassed to discuss it with my friends, so the burden was mine.

Since he first beat me, I could not have any conversation with him; if I did it ended up in a beating. He was a totally different man. I hated myself. I felt useless. I was ashamed of myself. There was only one girl I could share my problems with at work. My secret best friend was Kate; she could sympathize with me but could not understand why I stayed. Nobody could. I talked to a lady, seeking advice. She asked, "What do you mean you cannot leave? Does he lock up the doors? I think you too have a problem." From that day I decided I would never seek advice from anybody because they would just think I like to stay there to be thrashed.

In December of 1992 he told me we would go to his home village to see his parents. For the year we had stayed together, I had not met his parents. I only met his brothers and sisters in Nairobi. They seemed to fear him except one brother who was always with him most of the time he was beating me. According to our Kikuyu tradition, when a girl starts living with a man, the man's parents are supposed to go to her parents immediately to report that they are the ones who have "stolen" their daughter. On such an occasion, the girl and the man are supposed to be there so they can confirm that they are living together and that they are not hiding anything. In my case it did not happen.

Traditionally, the girl is supposed to remain a virgin until she is married either in church, customary or legally. My family was not only concerned about this, but by his hurting me. They knew if anything happened to me, he would even deny he knew me. I was happy when he said we would meet his parents. On December 24, 1992, we left Nairobi for Nyeri and his home. It is 150 kilometers from Nairobi. With the poor roads, it took two hours. His parents were happy to see us and were most welcoming. From that day I liked his parents and up to now still remember them fondly.

The following day was Christmas Day. We woke early and started cooking. People in Kenya, especially in the villages, need not be invited for Christmas. They just call in at lunchtime to wish their neighbors a merry Christmas. So you must cook lots of food. Lunch is served between 1 and 3, but people can eat any time. When neighbors call in, you do not even ask if they want food. That is rude. You just put food on a plate and after food you serve tea, whether it is lunchtime or suppertime. Pop or juice is a luxury, which is only afforded by few people, but at Christmas most people have those luxuries. You do not give people water unless they ask for it, otherwise they will say you are rude. We had many guests at that time since word had gone round that JB was bringing a girl home. In addition to coming because it was Christmas, our visitors also wanted to meet me.

When most of the visitors left at 5 p.m., my mother-in-law (unlike in North America, in Kenya you do not address your husband's parents or your wife's parents by name, you must call them Mom or Dad) said she wanted to talk to me. We sat in the kitchen. Typically in Kenya in the villages, there is a main house where there is a living room and bedrooms only. The kitchen is built as a separate house outside of the main house. The bathrooms are usually outside; as in the villages there is no piped water in houses. Women and children usually stay in the kitchen; there is a saying that a woman's place is in the kitchen.

JB, his father, and some male visitors were in the living room drinking beer. My mother-in-law asked me about my family, where I came from, what I did, and many other questions. I told her everything. Then she asked me how long I had lived with her son. I told her one-year. She asked me whether everything was going well between us. I started crying. She knew something was wrong. She asked, "Does he hurt you?" I told her yes. She hugged me and told me she was very sorry. I asked her why she had asked and she said because he used to do that to his first wife. That was a shock! He had never told me he had been married. I felt cheated. I went to our bedroom and lay down. After thirty minutes I heard him shouting and banging the wall, asking his mother where I was. I was terrified. He came to our room and asked me to open the door or he would break it.

When I opened the door, he started hitting me, accusing me of having a big mouth. (I realized later on that his mother had asked him why he hurts me). When he hit me, I was not supposed to cry for help or to get angry after the abuse. I was supposed to act as if everything was normal. Since I knew there were people there, I screamed and his father came to my rescue. He tried stopping him and in the process, I ran to the sitting room where the visitors were. The visitors could not understand and felt very bad. They had to leave. I went on the other side of the table; for him me to reach me; he climbed over the table and jumped over to where I was. He liked hitting me on the head more than any other part of the body. He used to tell me that he hit me on the head because I had no brains but water. I almost believed that I had no brains!

His mother started screaming, pleading with him not to kill me. After a beating, I always felt I had had an accident. My whole body ached. But the pain I felt in my heart was more than what I felt in my body. When his father told him what he did was bad, he told him that if he thought he could treat me any better, he was free to marry me. According to Kikuyu customs, one is not supposed to be rude to their parents, but JB never cared.

Later that night when we went to bed, he raped me violently. I do not know what pleasure he derived by raping me after he had abused me. I never enjoyed sleeping with him anymore. I hated him with all my heart. I just wished him dead! I wanted to talk to my parents and tell them what he did to me at his parents' house. I wanted them to know of his dishonesty, that he had another wife. After the 1993 New Year, we went back to Nairobi.

The Abuse Deepens

The following Monday we were going back to work. I had lots of bitterness. He was a fast and careless driver; I wished we had a terrible accident and died. Life had lost meaning for me. When we reached home that evening he apologized for hurting me in his parents' house and promised he had made it his new year's resolution to never hurt me again. He said he had realized his mistake and he pleaded with me not to leave, as he was tired of running after me. I could not believe he could apologize. For the first time after beating me almost twice a month since April of 1992, an apology? He made me to promise I would never leave. My face was still swollen and I had a black eye.

I knew he was trying to trick me. That was why he was forcing me to promise. He knew I would leave. That day after work I rushed back home, packed a few clothes, and went to my parents. They were used to it and it was like they were waiting for me any time. I told them how he beat me in his parents' presence and that it was impossible for them to stop him. My father said no matter what happened I was not to go back to him. Before we left his home, his parents had talked to me and pleaded with me that I should not tell anybody what had happened because it was the most embarrassing thing they had ever seen and they did not want anybody else to know, including my parents. I promised that I was not going to say a word to anybody. They said they were going to caution their son against hurting me again. They also said that forgiveness was the key thing and if I did not forgive their son, they would have a bad reputation among their neighbors.

The following day, I was afraid he would wait for me at work as he always did. He used a different trick. He called one of my work colleagues and asked if I had told her anything and whether she knew where I was. He kept calling until I arrived at work. When I answered the phone and I heard it was him, I hung up. He came to my office. I knew he would so I told the security officers at the door to tell him I had left. He was not convinced. He camped there the whole day until it was time to go home.

I was very scared and so I asked Kate to walk with me to the bus stop. Hardly had we walked five hundred meters from the office, when JB grabbed me from the back. I screamed. I was terrified. He asked Kate to go away. I was determined to leave him. I told him if he tried any games I would scream. He pleaded with me to go back home but I refused. He said how bad he felt because of what he did to me. He said even if it meant him bringing his parents to apologize to me and to my parents, he was ready to do so. I thought he was serious. This was on a Tuesday. The following Saturday, he came home with his parents. They apologized on behalf of their son and said they did not know what had gone wrong with him because he was a peaceful person. My mother asked them if they were aware of how many times he had hurt me. They promised they would talk to him and find out what the problem was. His problem was that he suffered from an inferiority complex and wanted to prove himself. Unfortunately, he could only do that by hurting the women in his life.

My parents warned him that if he ever hurt me again, they would not allow me to go back to him. We went back home. That was in January 1993.

By mid February of the same year, he had beaten me again. We came home from work and I was tired and feeling sick. I told him I could not cook because I was feeling sick and wanted to rest in bed before cooking. Most Kenyan men do not cook and the ones who cook are ridiculed by their friends and relatives, saying that their wives control them. He said I was pretending and started hitting me. I did not know what happened as I passed out. I came to later that night to find him holding my hand. I think this time he got scared and probably thought I would die. I asked him what happened and he said I should rest and I fell asleep. I slept without food until the following day. I was tired and weak from the beating. I realized that I was pregnant when I had a miscarriage the following day. It was painful. I was five weeks pregnant. When I started breeding profusely at night, he took me to the hospital. The doctor said that I had a miscarriage. When the doctor asked what happened, he lied and said I had fallen after fainting. He caused me lots of trouble later by telling me that I was barren and could not conceive and even if I conceived I was too weak to carry a pregnancy full term. After that miscarriage, he said he was not interested in children and so I could start taking birth control pills.

I took one week off work as the doctor advised me to have bed rest. I did not tell my family or friends. I was embarrassed and wondering if there was something wrong with me. I decided to seek a counsellor's advice without my husband's knowledge. I could not go because he was stalking me, and sometimes he could send people to stalk me. When I called my brother's wife, Njeri, and asked her if she knew a counsellor who could help, she gave me a name and telephone number. I called the counsellor and explained my problems; she said my husband had a serious problem and if I did not leave him sooner than later, he would do something really terrible to me. She said the choice was mine—stay and die or try to escape and risk his wrath. If I ran away I had no more ideas where I could go.

Before I hung up she told me; "If a man hits you once, he will never stop. If he has hit you more than ten times in less than two years, you are lucky to be alive. Pack up your things and leave now!" This was easier said than done. The worst problem I had was that nobody seemed to understand that I could not leave him. People were wondering how I could be forced to stay in a marriage I did not want.

That time I did not even attempt to leave. I had given up. I knew even if I did, I was not going to go far so I decided to hang in there. I was just praying that he would change and stop hurting me. The only thing that I decided to do was to accept the reality of staying and letting nature take its course. I had done my best but this was just not working. I was helpless and entirely at his mercy. Sometimes he could change for a few days, less than a week, and would become really good. This was always short lived and it scared me. He always came back with a greater force.

In July 1993 my niece Lilly whose mom had died sent me a letter, asking me to see her in school. She was in form one (grade nine in North America) in a boarding school. Sometimes I could not understand or believe what was happening in my life. I do not know how I kept my sanity for all those years. I got paid every month and did not have any money. When I received the letter, I called JB for some money so I could see my niece over the weekend. He said we would talk about it in the evening. After work he came to pick me up. This was unusual and I suspected all was not well. He held my hand and forced me into the car and told me that this was my last day. He used to make me freeze to such an extent that I could not scream or attempt to run.

We drove to a restaurant, ordered some food, and he said the reason we were there was for me to have my last supper and that he wanted to know the truth of where I wanted to go the following day. I told him the truth was simply the letter from my niece. It showed it to him, still in its postmarked envelope. He could not believe me. He said he would make sure I told him the truth and that he would teach me never to lie again.

When the food was brought, I told him I did not want eat it. He grabbed one of the plates with hot meat and hit me on the head. It was very painful because the food was steaming hot. Some people came to my rescue. He grabbed my handbag and started pulling me toward the car. As I resisted, he tore at my clothes. He got into the car and sped off, leaving me without money, jacket, or shoes. When the manager asked who that was, and I told him, some people started to laugh, saying I did not know how to take care of my husband. A lady asked if I wanted to report the matter to the police and I agreed. They drove me to the Pangani police station where I recorded a statement. I was asked me to come back the following day to take them to where he lived. I wondered why they could not go after him that night, but police in Kenya are beyond questioning.

The people who took me to report offered to take me back to the hotel because I had no money and nowhere to go. In Nairobi it is risky for women to walk at night; chances of being raped are or even murdered are very high. The manager gave me a room in the hotel. It was a room where employees slept. It was not lockable from inside and when the hotel was closed, the manager came to share the bed with me. He wanted to rape me and I threatened him with screaming if he tried anything. He got angry and threatened to kick me out of his hotel. I got out of bed and sat in the bathroom until morning. It was very cold as the bathroom was outside. When daylight finally came, I decided to go to my parents' place. I had no money for bus fare, not even enough to reach the city center. It was a very cold Saturday morning and don't forget, I had no shoes or sweater. I decided to walk downtown where I could request the drivers who operated the taxis to my hometown to drive me home and my parents would pay. It was a forty-five minute walk.

When I reached the bus stop I found a driver I knew well and told him my problem. The taxis go by queue and his was far. He gave me 100 shillings and said I could pay him back. When I reached home my mother started crying, saying that one-day JB was going to kill me. My father was very sad. Mom made me a hot cup of tea after which I showered. I put on one of my old dresses and my mother gave me a pair of shoes. My brother Peter (God rest his soul in eternal peace) was home for the weekend. When I told them what had happened Peter offered to accompany me to the police station. At noon we presented ourselves at the Pangani police station and told the policeman on duty why we were there. He said it was a family affair and that I should go home and sort it out with my husband. I later learnt that JB had already gone to the police station and bribed the officer in charge. The case was dropped.

The officer on duty said he had reported to work that morning and was acting on orders from above. That is the order of the day in Kenya—police always act on orders from above. You wonder whether *above* is heaven or Mars. My brother said he would take me to the house to pick up my clothes and make sure JB did not hurt me. We boarded a taxi to the house where we found JB with his brother and another man. They were happy, as if celebrating something. They were already drunk. Out of fear, I opted to remain outside as my brother went in. My brother convinced me that everything would be fine and that I should not fear. I followed him into the house and begged JB for my handbag and office keys. He refused, took my hand and dragged me into the bedroom where he locked me up. My brother could not believe what he saw. He asked my brother to join him for a drink but he refused. He said I was his wife and he had all the rights to do whatever he pleased. I cried out to my brother for help but he could not do much because he could not break the door to get me out. After staying there for almost three hours, my brother had no alternative but to leave. The most frustrating thing was that JB could mistreat me as members of my family watched but they could not help me or even get the police to help me.

After my brother left, JB asked how many men I slept with the previous night, and then beat me up as his friend and brother watched. He locked the bedroom door and raped me. He dared me to report again to the police and we would see who was going to be locked up. I later learnt my lesson when I was locked in the police cells for running away from him in 1998. Once he threatened me with something, he was sure to implement it, even if it didn't happen for a long time.

He was always making new rules: I should never get into his car. He used my money to fuel and repair it (it was always breaking down), yet I had no right to get a ride in it. I was not supposed to reach home after him in the evening; if I did I would be beaten.

In December of 1993 we went back to his home village for Christmas. It was a must that Christmas was to be spent with his family as if I had no family. To him my family did not exist. I used to miss my parents but there was nothing I could do because by that time we had even stopped going to visit them. That Christmas was better than the previous one because it went without incident. I had learnt my lesson from the previous year and had learnt to keep to myself. The insecurity JB had was so much that he was even insecure with me talking to his mother or his relatives. If he heard me or found his mother talking to me, even as we prepared the meals, he would just make rude comments like, "Women are women whether they are one year old or eighty years old, their work is to gossip." He would ask his mother what I was telling her and she would say we were just discussing the food we were cooking and nothing more.

This was exactly two years since we started staying together. Just hearing his footsteps or his voice could make me freeze to such an extent that something could drop from my hands. I could feel a chill all over my body. He knew I feared him and seemed to enjoy it.

Degradation,
Bryan is Born

For New Year's 1994 we went back to Nairobi. The more I feared him, the happier he was. I believed that each time he wanted me to be afraid of something new. When he made a new rule, he knew it was going to shake me for a while before I got used to it. When we got home he asked me why I was not getting pregnant. He knew very well I was on birth control pills because he had said he did not want my babies. When I reminded him of that he beat me. For the first time in all the beatings he had beaten me, I did not feel any physical pain. I was very angry. I stayed still as he beat me. I did not utter a word. I did not cry. When he hit me and I fell, I would sit up and wait for him to hit me even harder. Deep in my heart, I knew I was not going to stand it any more. I had reached the end. I was hopeless and more desperate than ever before. I wanted to die and knew that would be the end of my problems.

When we went to bed that night, he raped me as usual. That time he said he was out to make a baby. I knew I was not going to get a baby right away because I had taken a birth control pill the previous night. I did not mind getting children if that was going to change the situation.

When I went to work the following day, I made up my mind to run away. I thought it would be better to say in a hostel, than to go to my parents. As I did not have any money I asked my boss if I could get my salary in advance. Every time I made a decision to move out, I was determined not to return. My boss feared for me and asked if I thought it was a wise decision because he knew JB would come for me again. I told him I was not sure but at that moment I just wanted to get out of his life. I got my advance and called the Young Women's Christian Association hostel. It was a ten-minute walk from my office. They said they had space but I was required to sign some papers and make payments if I wanted to move in the same day. I walked there and after paying and signing the papers, took a taxi home, packed a few clothes, and went back to work.

At 5 p.m. I was ready to go to my new home. I had lots of confidence and apart from my boss, had not told anybody. I delayed in the office, as I did not want my colleagues to see me carrying a bag. The moment I stepped out of the office entrance, JB grabbed me from behind. I almost fainted. All my confidence, money, and efforts had gone to a waste again. I was not able to talk to him. As usual, somebody had followed me the whole day so JB knew exactly what I had done. He said we had to go home so that I could tell him what I had done during the day. I knew he would beat me to death. I was scared and sometimes I thought he could read my mind. I told him everything, but still he maintained I was lying. Surprisingly, he did not beat me. I got even more scared because I thought he was thinking of something worse than a beating. He said the next time I attempted to do something silly like that; I would know exactly what he was talking about. He took a kitchen knife. I went down on my knees to plead with him not to kill me. He lit the gas stove, and the once blade was red hot; he cut the upper part of my right hand. It was a deep, painful cut. That scar is still visible. He said that was just a small lesson and if I did not learn from that, next time he would teach me a better one. The wound became septic and took a long time to heal. He warned me against seeking medical treatment.

In Nairobi, you can walk into some pharmacies and buy an antibiotic. Since he took the rest of the money I had borrowed from the office, I had no money for drugs. I called my brother Tom and I asked him for some money, as I needed to buy drugs urgently. I did not tell him what had happened. He asked but I refused to tell him.

In March of 1994, JB was transferred to another government department. Since he was an auditor, he and some other people in the accounting department were stealing a lot of money from the government. He had so much money he was drinking every day and sleeping out almost every night. He started to infect me with sexually transmitted diseases. It was painful and when I told him, he would beat me and say I was sleeping with other men and bringing diseases home.

That April he was worse than ever. One morning he called me in the office. He had not been home for three days. He told me he was giving me exactly three months to conceive or I was going to pay for it. That time I got the courage to ask him, how he expected me to conceive if he was not even sleeping at home. He got mad and said he would answer that question later. I knew I would get

45

a real answer; sure enough, when he came home he beat me.

The following day, my employer was changing the staff identification cards and we needed pictures taken. I had braids on my hair, which had lasted for a while. At lunchtime, I went to the hairdressers to make my hair. I had nice long hair and when JB came home in the evening, he asked me why I had made my hair and where I got the money. That was the balance of the money my brother Tom had given me to buy drugs for my hand. I could not tell him where I got the money. He accused me of sleeping with men to get money to make myself beautiful. He searched my handbag for money but did not find any.

By June of the same year, he was sleeping at home twice or once a week. He had a girlfriend for whom he had rented a house in a plush area in Nairobi. I was so happy when he did not come home. I could sleep in peace. With all the money he had, he would not even buy a better car. He was still driving a junk. He would not buy good furniture for our house. He used to give his money and my money to his girlfriend.

One Friday evening in July he came home. I was lying on the couch watching television. He asked me to get up because he was taking me out that night, something he never did. I got scared. He was usually with three other men he used to work with. By now, JB had stopped eating at home; most of the time I went hungry because I had no money for food.

I could not question him or refuse, so I dressed and followed him to the car. He said we were going to his other wife's house. She was drinking with two other girls.

He introduced me as Njeri but did not say who I was to him. They started kissing and holding each other in my presence. It was very hurtful and I got really angry. I stood up, grabbed my handbag and as I made for the door, he held me and hit me really hard. He beat me and those girls started cheering him. It was so intimidating and painful. Those girls made fun of me and laughed at me. Within a few minutes, his drinking buddies and workmates came in. The girls were their girlfriends. They found me crying. They were shocked to see me there. They were married men too but at least they were not wife batterers. One asked JB what I was doing there and why I was crying. He said his girlfriend had wanted to see me and I was misbehaving so he decided to teach me a lesson! He told him, "JB you have been my friend and I respected you because I thought you were a sensible person. From today on, I will never talk to you. You have done something very inhuman to this girl. She does not deserve what you have done to her. I am out of this place and I will never come back again." He left. He meant what he said and never talked to JB again.

The following Monday, Eddy telephoned me at work. He said how sorry he was and did not know that JB was that kind of a person. He said somebody had told him he was abusing me but he did not think it was to that extent. He asked if there was any help I needed, I told him I was fine. After the incident at his girlfriend's house, he did not talk to me for a while. Then one evening he came home and said that he had confirmed that I could not conceive and so he wanted me to go for an x-ray, which he had booked at one of the medical centers in the city. He told me the appointment time and date. It was to be done after 5 p.m. I was not afraid because I knew I could conceive. That x-ray was painful. They had to insert something to check my uterus. It was the most uncomfortable thing I had gone through. JB had asked the doctor to call him with the results; of course, JB did not tell me the results. He continued to pressure me about getting a baby. He started to accuse me of taking birth control pills secretly. When I told him it was not easy to get a baby under pressure, he would beat me.

One evening around 4:30 p.m., my brother Tom happened to be in the building where JB worked. As he was heading for the elevator he met JB, who invited him to his office. JB telephoned and asked me to pass through his office as Tom was there so I could see him. I was glad because I had not seen my brother for a while. I found them talking about typewriters. Tom said he was looking for an IBM typewriter because his secretary had told him that they were good. I said I agreed with her because IBM were modern and had memories. I did not know or think that to talk in support of anybody else apart from him was an offence. After a few minutes Tom left.

JB's office was on the eighth floor; he locked the door and told me it was time for him to throw me out of the window. He started beating me, accusing me of making him look like a fool in front of my brother. After beating me to his satisfaction, he locked me inside and went away. After twenty minutes, I picked up the phone, dialled one of the extensions listed on the telephone; somebody picked up the phone and I told him I was in JB's office, that he had beaten me and locked me in there and left. He asked me who I was to JB. When I told him, he said since I was his wife, JB was free to do whatever he pleased. He hung up. I was desperate. I thought of calling the police but knew they would just make fun of me.

I knew God was the only one who could save me. I prayed to God that He would bring JB back and that he would not hurt me again. At 8 p.m., he came back. He gave me twenty shillings and asked me to go to a restaurant opposite his office, have a cup of coffee (nothing else!) and bring the balance of the money to him, together with the bill. I did not understand why, but without question, I did as told. I ordered the coffee, sat in the restaurant for a while, but did not even sip it. It was past 9 p.m. He asked me to catch a bus home and cook for him. He made sure I only had enough money to get home. When he arrived, I was in the middle of cooking. He asked me to turn off the stove and follow him to the bedroom.

He asked me to remove my clothes and get down on my knees, tell him how sorry I was for being a bad girl and that I loved him and would always love him and never leave him. You may think me silly, but I did that. It was very annoying. Since that day, it was like he discovered something new and every time he beat me I had to go down on my knees and repeat those silly words! I don't know if you will agree with me that forgiving such a person is almost impossible. I did forgive him but I will never forget. Forgiving him does not mean I could to go back and live with him or even talk to him. No. Ladies, be careful with that handsome man you are dating. You do not want to end up like me.

One Saturday in August 1994 JB came home earlier than normal. He went straight to bed without saying a word. After a few minutes he called me. I feared he was going to beat me up. Surprisingly, he was very polite. He asked me to sit on the bed. He said there were some people he owed some money and they had sent word that if he did not pay them that day, they would kill him. In my heart I just prayed they would. That would be the end of my troubles! I asked him how much money and he said Kenya Shillings 70,000. I asked how he got the money and for what, he turned wild and told me to shut up. He instructed me not to answer the door and that I should turn out the lights and go to bed. I did. In less than half an hour, hell broke loose in our house. People started banging on the door, threatening to break the door if we did not open. I got very scared and told him I would scream for help. He warned me if I screamed I would pay dearly for it. In Nairobi, if someone says they will kill you, they usually carry out their threat.

In Nairobi most doors are made of steel because of the crime rate. I ran from the bedroom to the kitchen window where I could see them. They asked me to open the door but I refused. I told them I was not going to do that and they should stop banging the door because I was not there when JB borrowed the money. A man said he heard what I was saying but they had to get either their money or they would kill him. I pleaded for a few more days. He said he sympathized with me because he knew where JB had taken the money. He said they would go but come back the following day at 7 a.m. and if he tried to hide, they would get him.

When I went back to the bedroom JB was so scared that he could only whisper. For once, he thanked me for saving him. I thought of telling him that was how scary it was when somebody says they would hurt you. I stopped because I knew what would happen if I said something like that to him. The guys kept their word. At 7 a.m. the following day they were at the door. I wished they could beat him but not kill him so he could feel the pain of being hurt. He was fortunate enough to convince them he would get them their money the following day, which was a Monday. I heard them tell him they would go to his office at lunchtime to pick it up. He must have paid them because I did not see them at our home again. It was not a very good experience. A similar incident happened in 1998 when he refused to pay rent for a couple of months.

By September of 1994, I was getting very lonely because most of the time I was at home alone. I started praying to God to give me a baby. I was thinking that if only I could get my husband a baby he might be happy with me. When I got a baby and the situation at home did not change, but actually became worse, I learnt that with or without children, it did not matter. He was just using it as an excuse to terrorize me. I had two reasons why I desperately wanted a baby—to prove to my husband that I could have a baby and for the baby to keep me company. I also used to hear that nobody beats a pregnant woman so I knew if I got pregnant I could go for nine months without being hurt. I later realized this was a wishful thinking when I got pregnant and nothing changed.

By the end of November 1994, I started having morning sickness, so I went for a pregnancy test. I was very happy when the doctor told me it was positive. I thought this would make my husband happy.

By December, he was already tired of my morning sickness and being picky in what I ate. I could not stand most foods. He said I was pretending and thought I was the first one ever to get pregnant. He said he was waiting to see if I could carry that pregnancy full term because I was a weakling. I asked God to protect my baby and me and prove him wrong. I knew how much that baby would mean to me. At least I would have something to live for because life had lost meaning to me.

I received lots of support from my colleagues at work and my family. We went to their home again for Christmas of 1994. This was a routine that could not be changed. We reached Nyeri at 3 a.m. on December 25, 1994. When his parents knew we were coming home, they could not sleep no matter how late we arrived. They just sat and waited. In Africa, parents who have retired mostly depend on their children to help them with money. In this case, JB was the sole breadwinner and they used to treat him like a small god. He had the money to buy food and everything they needed. Even if they knew he was being mean to me, they could not confront him for fear of him not giving them money.

Christmas was as boring as usual to me. There was no more fun because I was always in fear. I missed the time I spent with my family. I did not do as much cooking as the previous Christmas; I was tired and sick. Christmas Day passed without incident and I spent most of the day in the bedroom.

The following day we went to visit his sister who lived in Kitale with her family. It was a very long journey especially if you just traveled from Nairobi, pregnant and not happy. It was 500 kilometers from Nyeri to Kitale.

We had a tire burst just before we reached Nakuru. We stopped there for more than an hour for the tire to be fixed and to have lunch. As usual, he was driving fast and carelessly. He used to pass, even when he did not have a clear view of oncoming traffic. One time he did that and we almost crashed into a bus. I was very scared and screamed. He got so mad with me he pulled off the road, leaped out, came around to my side, jerked open the door, pulled me out, and started beating me.

His father, mother, two brothers, and a sister were there. Nobody stopped him. I cried for help and that is when his father got out of the car and asked him to stop. He told his father he would stop when he felt like and that I was his wife and could do whatever he pleased. His mother pleaded with him to stop hurting me but he would not listen. She told him he could kill me or make me have a miscarriage if he continued to hurt me. He said he did not care and would be surprised if I carried the pregnancy to term. I wanted to run far away. We were in the middle of nowhere and it was getting dark. He forced me into the car and continued driving at high speed. Nobody said anything about that incident later. Another closed chapter.

We spent three long days at his sister's house. I just wanted to get out of there. The rest of her family had told her what happened on the way. It was my first time to meet her and so did not know what kind of a person she was. One afternoon her husband said he wanted to take us out. I said I was tired and wanted to rest. JB's sister said she would stay with me. I did not want to talk to her about anything even though she asked me why JB had beaten me on the roadside. I told her I did not wish to talk about it. She said she was sorry and all she would ask me was to be very careful with her brother because she had lived with him in Nairobi with the first wife and she witnessed how he used to mistreat her. I was tired of listening to things about him so I told her it was ok.

We went home on the third day. The driving was long, tiring, and scary. This time his father said he was going to sit on the co-driver's seat. We stayed at his parents' house until after the New Year when we went back to Nairobi.

I had lost so much weight that when I went to the antenatal clinic; the doctor recommended a scan to find out whether the baby was growing all right. He advised me to eat properly. I did not have money to buy the food for a proper diet. I now worked in a bank as an assistant to the head of operations. I was earning much more money than when we met. Things like fruit or milk were a luxury and since I did not have money, most of the time I used to go without lunch or proper meals.

One day in April 1995, it rained heavily; I telephoned JB from my office to request a ride home in his car. He refused, so I got onto a crowded bus. Usually, there are heavy traffic jams because everybody is rushing to go home. That day was no exception. There was a heavy traffic jam and by the time I reached home it was 9 p.m. and JB was already there with his brother. When he opened the door, he kicked me, hit my head with an umbrella, and locked me out. I was six months pregnant. I went to the neighbor's house and slept there. The following day I went home because I knew even if I did not he would still come for me.

On July 11, 1995 Bryan was born. The doctor said the baby needed to be treated for stress. After a week in hospital, we were discharged; JB seemed to have changed. He bought food and came home early. For the rest of the year he did not hurt me. I thought that it was true that children bring happiness to marriages. We went to church as a family and even made arrangements for Bryan to be baptized. Christmas of 1995 we went to his home village as usual. He was very helpful with the baby and did not mistreat me at all.

Escape, Recapture, Police Abuse

When we went back to Nairobi in January 1996, he was still a good husband and a responsible father. We could chat and sit at the table together for dinner and breakfast. He could give me money to buy food for the baby and to pay the babysitter. In Africa, when you have children, you employ a maid to live with you, to do housework, and take care of the children while you go to work. We often went to visit my parents; I told tell them things had really changed and that my life was good. Little did I know that it was short lived.

In August of the same year JB became more abusive and violent than ever. I could not survive anymore. He would beat me in the presence of my babysitter and my baby. Then he would turn on Bryan and slap him like you would a grown up when he cried. I could not stand it one more day, especially to watch him abuse a baby.

I decided to look for a house to rent for the baby, the maid, and myself. I took a day off from work, packed the baby's clothes and mine, and left. My maid, just like everybody else, could not understand why I just sat there and wait to be thrashed any time JB felt like it. I rented a one-bedroom house. I did not carry anything that he had bought. I had a couch, bed, and a few dishes. This was good for a start.

After we unpacked in the new house, I sat on the couch and cried. I was so glad I had at long last made it. I had never thought I would get such courage. Every time I left him, I was so convinced it was the end of my problems. The following day, my former boss who was a lawyer helped me to file for separation, for legal custody of Bryan, and a restraining order. They were granted. He was served with the papers and it made him even madder. The following morning he was at my office door. He had come with his brother and two other men. He threw me into a waiting truck; I screamed for help and one of my colleagues saw what happened. He ran to the office, informed my boss, and he immediately called my brother. They drove me to a forest and told me to say my last prayers unless I showed him where I was staying. I told him I would. He took the restraining order from his pocket, tore it into small pieces, and told me never to try anything like that again. A week after, I came home from work to find the house empty and that my son and the maid were nowhere to be seen. When I asked the neighbors, they said JB had packed everything into a truck, chased away the maid, and took the baby. By now he had lost his job and I was the sole breadwinner.

A few minutes later, JB showed up with his brother and told me to get in the car. I did because I knew resistance would only result in more suffering. He drove me to a house where I found my son with a newly hired maid. He told me this was our new home and I should never attempt to leave again and I should treat the new maid with lots of respect. Later I realized he was sleeping with the maid while I worked, since he was not employed.

From that time to 1997, the abuse was the same to the baby and me.

In March 1998, he got himself a well paying job with an international organization. Ironically, he was the finance manager of a project that was helping women to start self-help projects. He used to travel to North America and South America because they had offices in most countries in the world.

He got himself a small girlfriend who later went to the United States for further studies. That little girl could call my house and call me all kinds of names. When I asked him, he said I was the one making the phone calls to her and he would beat me for that.

One day in August 1998, I found a letter on the bedroom table, which he may have left there by mistake. The little girl's father had sent it to him. I call her *little* because she was in her very early twenties. The girl's father was thanking him for all the financial help he had given his daughter and his family. He said it was for the good of JB and Bridgette that she had gone to study in the United States. He may join her or when she came back to Kenya, they would get married. I carried the letter to work and made a photocopy. When he came back home in the evening I gave him the original. That was the worst mistake I had ever made!

He went berserk and went into the kitchen and removed a bottle of beer from the fridge. He opened it and started drinking; all hell broke loose when he threw the bottle at me and missed by inches. The bottle hit the wall and beer and glass flew everywhere. Bryan was four years and he feared JB greatly. He held me and started crying, begging his father not to kill me. He stopped beating me and started to beat Bryan, telling him he was just like his mother. I thought he was going to kill him. I asked him to leave Bryan alone and beat me instead. When he was done with Bryan he started beating me. He forced me to clean up all the beer and glass with my bare hands. I got several cuts.

That night I thought I would run away and stay with a friend he did not know. I could not go to work the following day because of the cuts on my hands and pain in my body. I called a friend when JB went to work and asked if she could accommodate my son and me for two weeks until I decided what to do. She agreed. This was a secret friend and JB did not know her. I packed a few things and we left. For one whole week, he did not look for me. Surprisingly he knew where I was and was just taking his time because he knew he was going to come in a big way. When he hurt me and I could not make it to work, my maid used to go to the telephone booth to call my boss to inform them that I was sick.

Before you read what I experienced in the Kenya police cells where my "loving " husband had me locked up for a week, I would like you to read the following report in a Kenyan newspaper about the conditions of police cells in Kenya.

03/02/2005

Crime Suspect's Worst Nightmare

Police cells, generally thought to be crime-free zones, may be as dangerous as the most dreaded urban back street.

One may escape mugging in a dark Nairobi alley but would have to be really fortunate to avoid robbery in the cell—at the very best—or sodomy at worst.

In most of the cells, male and female inmates are crammed into tiny rooms adjacent to toilets and bathrooms where rape and sodomy and many indignities are committed on newcomers by those locked up for long periods or those who frequent the places.

Investigations show that suspects who end up most tormented are those without money, for with it; one can live in relative comfort. A number of people who have passed through any of the police cells in Kenya have gruesome tales of torture and anguish at the hands of fellow inmates as police officers watch. If one fails to deposit their money with police at the report desk, the police officer escorts you to the cells and signals to the inmates who have been there for a long time to "take care of the guest."

This is a signal to terrorize you, for soon the other inmates grab you, wrestle you to the ground and relieve you of all your belongings. Some fondle your private parts pretending to be searching for valuables.

I was locked up in Kilimani police station in Nairobi for one week until I signed a document written by JB that I would go back home with him and never run away from home again. There were no charges laid. My crime: I had left an abusive husband.

My friend's house was located at Kibira, near the Kilimani police station. From 5 a.m. on that Saturday morning there were several phone calls in Njeri's house (we share the same middle name). People were calling, asking for me. I knew the worst had come. I was so afraid that I could not move because I knew he might have sent some people to surround the compound. At 6 a.m., we had a loud bang at the gate. People were shouting that if we did not open, they would break the gate. By the time Njeri went to open the gate, JB had already jumped over the gate and was right in the house screaming for my blood. On opening the gate, there were five policemen, all armed with guns. JB's brother was with them—a total of seven men! JB stormed into the room where Bryan and I were and started beating me, right in front of the police. The police supported him by telling him I needed to be disciplined. They bundled my friend and I into a waiting police truck and drove us to Kilimani police station where JB gave the police instructions to "take care of us." He left with Bryan.

On weekends, police patrol the streets of Nairobi and arrest drunks and loiterers. If you are female and arrested, your charge is different from that of a man. Ladies are charged with loitering with immoral purposes with an intention of selling themselves. Men are charged with being drank and disorderly. The law allows this kind of discrimination. Both men and women are arrested at the same time for the same activity, but women are charged with the stronger charge of selling themselves. Prostitution is illegal in Kenya. So that Saturday we got many new arrivals. They were drunk, very happy, and kept singing their favorite songs. The room was crowded and stinking.

On Wednesday of the following week I asked a policewoman to call my brother and tell him where I was. When he came to see me, he was refused entrance. The police told him to leave or they would shoot him dead! In Kenya, if a police officer says he will shoot you, he will!

"Taking care of us," meant torture. At roll call, the police would kick me with their boots and I would go sprawling. They would then make fun of me, saying I was too weak and that was why my husband was beating me. My friend and I were made to clean the buckets and carry human waste. We did all that with bare hands—no gloves and no shoes. We slept on the hard and cold floor for one week until JB came to get us out. The condition? I had to sign a statement that I would never cause trouble by leaving my "loving husband" again. I had to sign for my friend's sake, the one who suffered so much simply because she had helped me. I did not see my son for the whole week.

From that day I said I would never attempt to leave him again, whether he hurt me or kill me. It was the worst thing he had ever done to me. What I went through at the hands of the police and the inmates will forever remain in my memory. All that time I was in the police cells, he was locking Bryan in the house the whole day without food or water until he came back from work. The neighbors later told me Bryan used to call out to people from the window to open for him.

There was a woman in the cells who seemed to have lived there the longest. She asked me why I was there and when I told her on my husband's orders, she replied, "Kill him." She was serious and offered to give me the telephone contacts and names of people who would do the job. I was afraid but that thought kept on crossing my mind. True, I met hard-core criminals in jail and true, being in jail is like being in training, but my Christian beliefs, my trust in God, and my conscience could not allow me to do it.

Between 1999 and 2001, whenever he hurt me, he would just remind me of the police cells. I knew he would make it happen and I was not ready to go through what I went through again. During that time, he started nagging me about another baby. Again I though if I got another baby for him, things might improve. I got pregnant in 2000, and he started hurting me more regularly than before. In February 2001 Bryan got sick with malaria; I told JB Bryan was sick and could not go to school. When he started beating me, I ran to the bathroom. He followed and Bryan came to my rescue asking him to "leave my mom alone." After Bryan turned four, he always fought JB when he hurt me. In return he would beat both of us. That day, he beat Bryan and he was sick, hit me so hard that I started bleeding. I was seven months pregnant. I was only wearing sleep wear and he removed it in front of my son and told him to see how ugly his mother was. That day I almost committed suicide. Thanks to my brother Ndaba and his wife Njeri, a friend took me to hospital and I lied to the doctor that I fell in the bathtub and that is when I started bleeding.

From that day, Bryan was reserved and talked very little. He lost weight, his grades deteriorated, and he complained of headaches. Sometimes he would have such severe headaches that sweat would drip from his forehead like water. He was so protective that sometimes, I would go to the bathroom and when I came out, find him sitting outside the bathroom door. When I asked why he said he did not want anybody to hurt me! I knew he was being affected psychologically when he started getting nightmares. He would scream, "Leave my mother alone! Don't kill my mother!" When I went to his room he was sweating and shivering. This became a great concern but I had no choice but to live with it. If his father happened to be home when this happened, he shouted at him and told him he was pretending and to go back to sleep.

Kevin is born

On April 25, 2001 Kevin was born. After that JB started to make fun of me—now that I had two boys, there was nowhere I could go. He was right. I had made up my mind: if that was the way my life was meant to be, so be it.

Around that time, he was dating Jessica. I think she really had made him crazy; she would come home with him and they would sleep in my bed. The baby and I would sleep in the maid's bedroom. Jessica used to call the house and ask for him and would even leave messages for him. One day I was hurt and decided to call her and give her a piece of my mind. I told her that any normal human being would not do what she was doing. She said I would pay for talking like that. JB came home that evening breathing fire! My niece Chiku was in my house that time. She had witnessed so much of the abuse that one day she told me she was going to kill him. I told her not to worry because I believed that one day all the problems I had would come to an end. JB called me to the bedroom. He hit me so hard across my face that I fell down. He beat me until he was satisfied. He then asked me to pick up the phone, call Jessica, and apologize. It was so humiliating; I hate myself today for doing it.

In December 2001, we went to Mombasa for a vacation. His employer treated managers and their families to a Christmas vacation. While there, he mistreated me so much that when I ordered food he told the waiter not to bring it. When his colleagues asked why he said I was his wife and he had a right to decide what I would or would not eat, even though the company was footing the bill. Mombasa, on the shores of the Indian Ocean, is hot and humid. I could not even wear a bathing suit because I had no permission to swim. When everybody else was out on the beach or swimming, I was supposed to stay in the hotel room.

After the vacation, we went to his home in Nyeri in January 2002. Bryan had stomach flu and when I suggested that we take him to the doctor, JB refused. Even if one of the boys had something as simple as a fever, I could not give him anything without JB's permission. If he was not home, I was supposed to call him for approval.

One morning, JB woke up very early and without saying a word to me, left. I learnt later in the day that he had told his family he was going to Nairobi. During the day, Bryan got very sick, so I called him on his cell to ask him to help take Bryan to the doctor. From their home to the main road where one can get public transport, it takes well over an hour to walk. When he heard it was me, he hung up. I was so frustrated with having an infant and a very sick six year old. JB's parents were not bothered about my son being sick.

At about 8 that night, I was in the bedroom, watching over Bryan and trying to make Kevin sleep. JB stormed into the compound like a mad man, hooting all the way from the gate to where he parked. I got so scared I started to sweat. He slammed the car doors, ran to the house, and demanded to know where I was. When his mother told him I was in the bedroom, he practically ran to the bedroom and without any warning, he started hitting me and calling me names. He demanded to know why I was calling him and why I had talked to my brother on the phone during the day. I tried to explain that Bryan was very sick and still needed urgent medical help. He told me he did not care if he died, as he was neither his first nor last son. That day Bryan was too weak to fight and all he did was cry. I ran to the sitting room, thinking his parents and relatives would help; he followed me. When I ran from one corner of the house to the other he smashed the coffee table into the wall, breaking it into pieces. He smashed all the plates on the sideboard by throwing them on the ground. He did the same to the cups, glasses, ashtrays, my cell phone, and anything else he could lay his hands on. When his dad told him to stop, he told his father he was stupid and old and did not understand anything. He said he wanted me to call my parents and tell them "they were senseless and stupid as they were the ones who were spoiling me and they should never talk to him." He forced everybody out so I could call from outside as there was no network in the house. I later learnt that his parents had supported him on this, since he had told them my parents had sent for them. He called my parents but I refused to talk to them. I told him that I would rather die than insult my parents. He threatened to drive me to my parents at that time of the night. I knew he was up to something. He either wanted to cause an accident and have me killed or would kill me on the way. I had never seen him as mad as that day. He was shaking and foaming from the mouth. His father told him if he took me to my parents, he could only so that during the day.

The worst happened when we went back to the house. He stripped me naked in front of his parents and family. He tied me on the bed with a rope, locked me in the bedroom, and carried the key with him until the following day. I could hear my children crying but I was helpless. When he came back in the evening of the following day, he opened the door and untied me. He asked me to apologize to him and to his family for being an embarrassment to them. I did so! How can anybody face his or her parents-in-law after an incident like that? I thought I would have to run away when we went back home, but did not know where to go because I was certain that he would come for me. I did not want a repeat of the police cells.

On January 07, 2002 we went back home. I did not go to work the following day, as my maid did not show up yet. JB pretended to be sick and stayed home. He looked suspicious and probably thought that I would take off. The following day I still had to stay home with Kevin. Bryan went to school and JB went to work. That is the time I thought and decided that it was my last day there.

Final Decision –
Women Shelter

On January 9, 2002 during the day, our security guard came to my house to ask if I needed a temporary maid because my maid had not reported yet. In Kenya women go knocking on doors looking for work. I agreed to employ her on a temporary basis as I was still expecting my maid to show up. That was the woman who helped me to escape by getting me a taxi downtown. There are no taxi companies in Kenya like in North America that you can pick up the phone and call for a cab.

On that day at 5:30 p.m., I left the home I had built for ten years—never to go back. I did not even look back and I never will—I left the door open, all the lights and the television on. Bryan was six and Kevin only eight months. I had paced up and down the whole day. I had not even had a drink of water. I was waiting for Bryan to come home from school and then we would go. I had one mission to accomplish that day—leave and never go back. I wanted to go to the Women's Rights Awareness Program—a battered women's shelter that was south from where I was. I found myself going east—I was determined to run.

I stood at my bedroom window waiting for the school bus. It was 4:35 when Bryan arrived. I raced downstairs and asked my new maid to quickly go to town and come back with a taxi, as there was a bag to be taken to the airport for somebody who was flying out. When Bryan came in, I was already packed. I could not carry much baggage because I had to carry the baby on my back and Bryan was still weak from the sickness. I told Bryan it was time we went very far away and he told me we should have gone a long time ago.

To escape, I used tactics to avoid confrontations with the security guard. JB had given him instructions that I should never leave home with the kids and bags, so I sent him to the shop. I gave him one hundred shillings and asked him to go to the other side of the road to buy some Coke. It had to be very cold and there was only one shop that had cold pop in that neighborhood. I knew it was going to take more than twenty minutes, so in his absence, the cab arrived and we took off. I have no idea what happened to or how he faced JB's wrath. I feel sorry for the security man.

We gave the maid a ride to her home and I paid her for the day and asked her to report to work the following morning as usual. I did not want anybody to suspect anything. All along the cab driver thought we were going to the airport. After we dropped the maid, I told him we were going to Kakamega, about thirty-eight kilometers. I had never been there before and did not know why I had selected this place. I asked the cab driver to drop us at a bus stop and come back after fifteen minutes. If he did not find us, he was free to go. I paid him the full amount. I wanted to confuse him because I knew he would later be in trouble if JB found out that he was the one who had driven us. It was dark and I did not know what to do or where to go with my children. I asked somebody if they could show us where to get public transport to Webuye. Don't ask why I selected Webuye, I don't know. All I knew—I was on the run! We got a taxi to Webuye; I had never been there before. It was a small, dusty, and dark town. We were stranded. I did not know which direction to go. A man noticed that I was stranded and asked if he could help. I told him we were there to visit my sister but I had lost her telephone number and since it was night time, I asked him to show us a hotel for the night. He helped me with the bag as I carried Kevin and held Bryan's hand. He took us to a hotel; we were lucky enough to get the last room. Unfortunately, customers had to identify themselves, so I had to show my identity card. I bought some fries for Bryan and some milk for the baby as I had instant food and a flask with hot water.

I did not sleep a wink that night. I woke the children at 6 and requested the hotel workers to show us where we could catch a bus to Nairobi. They showed us the bus stop and we booked our tickets. It was a long and tiring journey with a lot of thoughts and fear. We reached Nairobi on Thursday January 10, 2002. I dared not go to the city center for fear that JB had employed someone to look for us. I asked a cab driver to take us to the Women's Rights Awareness Program (WRAP) where we were cordially received by the co-ordinator. On realizing how stressed and tired I was, she booked us in and asked me to rest and that she would listen to my case the following day. That night I felt so secure—as there was a big fence and security guards at the gate, knowing they would not allow any people in without knowing who they were. We showered, had a good meal, and Bryan seemed very relieved and confident. This was very short-lived. Greater things were to come after JB realized we had been sheltered there.

The shelter found themselves in lots of trouble from JB and the police for all of 2002. Director Anne Ngugi (a woman of substance) was arrested a couple of times. She confessed later that in all her working life of helping battered women and children, she had never dealt with a case as bad as mine. JB was so intimidating that he would pay people to follow her vehicle everywhere. He made phone calls to her house day and night. When she reported him to the police, they were always on JB's side because he bribed them.

A letter dated March 7, 2002 from Women's Rights Awareness Program says it all.

On March 6 2002, at 10.30 am we were leaving for downtown. I was actually in the vehicle; I heard a loud bang at the gate. I turned around and saw people coming through the smaller gate and at the same time our security man was forcing them out. Those outside pushed with great force and in came people armed with AK47 rifles. I ran inside and then outside again in a matter of seconds by which time the gate had been flung open and there was a white Peugeot KAM station wagon parked at our gate. There were a total of nine men and one lady six of which were armed. Standing tall and smiling was JB, Njeri's husband. I went towards them. They had already severely beaten our security personnel with blows, kicks and the baton of the rifles. They told me I was under arrest and I had to accompany them to Kilimani Police Station. At the police station I was told that JB had filed a complaint of abduction and kidnapping of his wife

and two children and I was demanding from him
Kenya Shillings half a million.

Anne Ngugi, Director,
Women's Rights Awareness Program.

That is the kind of police brutality in Kenya. They always side with rich husbands because they always bribe them. How can a woman who runs a bartered women shelter abduct my children and I where as the records indicated that I had left the shelter? No matter how much my family tried to convince the police that they knew where I was it fell on deaf ears. If you do not have money in Kenya especially where the law and the police are concerned, nobody will listen to you. The law of the jungle is what is mostly practiced in Kenya – the law of money – money talks.

I had to move from one place to another, sometimes at night with my children. I did not know that one day I would be a free woman. Today I know what it means to be free from spousal abuse and what it means to be a spouse slave or prisoner. That man sentenced me to life imprisonment with no option of a parole; he had vowed that death was the only thing that would ever separate us. By the way, I was never legally married to him. A law in Kenya says, "When a man and a woman live together for two years, they are automatically declared husband and wife." I am still doing research on whether there is a law that says, "If they are separated for two years, they are declared divorced."

The following day was Friday, January 10, 2002. I went to see Lisa the coordinator. After listening to my story, she re-assured me I was very safe and that they were protected by the government and as long as I was in that compound, nothing should worry me. I left her office unconvinced! The whole day I was trying to figure out what or where to go next, as that was not a permanent solution to my problems. Bryan was to be in school and that was important to me. On Saturday night JB started calling WRAP and asking to talk to me. The staff had been asked not to disclose to anybody that I was there. The receptionist said she did not know me, but he kept calling until she turned off the phone. On Sunday morning she told me all was not well; JB had obtained information from the telephone company about the calls I had made on the day I left him. I had talked to a lawyer at the Federation of Women Lawyers Kenya who had directed me to WRAP. That lawyer also had her share of troubles from JB. I insisted to the social worker we must call the director and ask if she could help me by taking me to a different shelter. When we talked to the director she took it casually and said she would see me the following day, Monday, in her office and there was no cause for alarm. I told her JB was a bad person but she said she had seen worse men and there was nothing to fear. She believed me later when she met JB in real life and was terrorized for one full year until she had to move the women's shelter to a different location.

The whole of Sunday my children and I never left the room. We could not even go to the dining room. First thing on Monday I went to the director's office and asked her either to believe what I was telling her or hell would break loose there. She paid attention to what I said about my marriage and she seemed to understand. She asked if I was ready to put it down in writing. I told her I did not have a problem with that. For the first time in ten years, somebody was paying attention, had time to listen, believed me, and agreed to help. She put me in front of a computer and after reading my report again and again, she told me she was going to look for a place to relocate us. I was relieved but warned her to be very careful because she might suffer the consequences for helping us. I asked if she noticed in my statement that one of my friends had been jailed for helping. She said that could never happen to her because she was helping a number of women and children and her organization was registered with the government.

Flee, A police helicopter

On Monday, January 14 I signed a form at WRAP indicating that I had left. Before leaving, I warned them I was sure JB would go there and when he did, he would enter either through the gate or jump over it if the guards refused him entry. It happened a few days later.

The director took us to another shelter, about thirty kilometers from Nairobi. We arrived past working hours and a housekeeper who did not know her job booked us in. After an hour, the director came and said that they do not accept women with sons over five. Bryan was six; so we had to be sleep in a kindergarten classroom which that organization was running. She asked me to call whoever took us there the following day to come pick us up. The following morning I went to her office and told her I was not leaving for a few days. She thought I was kind of crazy. She asked what my problem was and I told her I did not wish to discuss it with her but the most important thing was that I would not leave! That was real trouble! The classroom had only one small mattress. I had a baby wrapper and a shawl to cover my children. The room had no windowpanes and mosquitoes were like flies. The mattress was so small that Bryan had to face one side and Kevin the other. I slept on the floor.

That shelter was for women going through rehabilitation. Some had been on drugs, others suffered from chronic diseases. Most had children who were under six years. On day two, Bryan was playing outside with some other kids, when he noticed a police helicopter. He went flat on his stomach—he thought his father was looking for us. When it flew away, he ran to me, sweating and panting. I asked what the problem was and when he told me, I told him not to worry because I did not think JB could go to such an extent.

I realized we were not safe there when one of the women called me by name. I was not using my real name so this was a real shock. I called Anne and told her we had to leave that place immediately. Kevin was sick with malaria; it is a disease that can kill if untreated for a few days. Anne sent another lady and a taxi driver for us. We were taken to a highly populated estate in Nairobi called Kayole. From that day to the day I landed in Canada I covered my head and part of my face with a veil so people would not recognize me.

On January 22, 2002, Anne asked me to call Judy Thongori of the Federation of Women Lawyers (the lawyer who had given me the contact for WRAP) because JB was harassing her very much. When I called Judy, she was shocked to hear that I was safe and not sick. JB had convinced her that I suffered from mental illness and said he was worried I might harm the children or myself. His prayer to her was to help him get me back home. Judy advised me to call JB and assure him we were safe. He knew I had talked to Judy because again he tracked the numbers I had called the day I left. I used a telephone booth to call him at work at exactly 3.22 pm on January

22 2002 and I told him; "This is the last time you will ever hear my voice on the phone or in person." I hung up and have never talked to him again and I will never. I did not give him a chance to say anything.

On January 30, 2002 JB, in the company of two police officers—Mr. Wamuayi from the criminal investigation department in Kisumu and Mr. Njuguna from the Kilimani police station walked into the Women's Rights Awareness Program offices. JB went directly to where the women and children slept and conducted an unlawful search in front of his cop friends, lifting the clothes, mattresses, and blankets in the presence of the women and children who had sought shelter.

The Women's Rights Awareness Program director and employees were taken to Kilimani police station and after recording statements were released. Even after complaining to the commanding officer about the unlawful search and harassment by JB, they were dismissed by him saying that JB had a right to search for his wife and children anywhere and anytime he pleased. It was legal because I was his property.

Hiding in Uganda

After the director and her employees were released, we agreed I had to leave the country as soon as possible, realizing JB would eventually get us with the help of the police. That evening we took a bus to Uganda, the only place we could go without passports. We could get a temporary pass at the boarder. Fortunately, I had my passport and the children were endorsed. With Nairobi traffic a perpetual twenty-four hour mess, it took us well over an hour to reach the bus station. The bus to Kampala was full, so I asked if there was another bus going to any other part of Uganda. There was one going to Mbale, 300 kilometers from Kampala. I had never been to Uganda and had no idea where Mbale was, but I bought tickets anyway. When I went to the ticket office, I had left the children with Patricia in the taxi. I was looking over my shoulder in case JB or his agents were lurking around. When I went back to the taxi, I could not find it. I thought the driver and Patricia had colluded to steal my children. I had friends who had fallen victim to JB's sweet talk and money and they had betrayed me. One time he confessed to me that he was such a sweet talker that he could sweet talk a snake out of its hole. After five minutes of frantic looking, I saw them approaching. Patricia said they had to move because of parking rules. What a relief!

We arrived at the Kenya/Uganda border at four in the morning; to get across, I said we were going to attend my sister's wedding and that we would be in Uganda for two weeks. It was easy to get a two-week visa but I stayed for a year.

A friend of a friend (who became "my auntie" and who is still scared of JB) helped us. The agreement was that I was to live in my house and she would help me find one. I had no problem with that as long as I got as far as possible from JB. We reached Mbale February 1 and our long journey started. Language was a problem because most people spoke Luganda—of which I did not know a word—when they realized I was not Ugandan, anything I wanted to buy suddenly cost three times the regular price. I had never been out of my country, so it was frustrating to always being called a foreigner and treated with suspicion. I bought milk and bread and got into a taxi, which was to take us to Kampala where we had to meet Auntie.

We reached Kampala in 35 degree heat. I had a bag, a baby on my back, and had to hold Bryan's hand. We went to the nearest telephone booth and called Auntie. Within a few minutes she came; she was so kind to us. We went to the Kampala YWCA for temporary accommodation before we got our own house. When the receptionist learned we were from Kenya and were seeking accommodation for a few days, she said that since we were foreigners, we had to pay in U.S. dollars! I only had little money and when we calculated the cost for three days, it was a lot of money, without the cost of food. Auntie was kind enough to accommodate us in her home as we looked for a house.

The following day being a Saturday, she decided to help me look for a house. She called one of her friends; who said that there were nice houses in a shopping center near where she lived. We went, saw the house, and I had no choice but to rent it because I didn't want Auntie to think I was out to use her by staying in her house for free. The front was a shop and the back was one room. There were no people in the other shops and when I asked why all the other houses were vacant, the landlord said he was renovating the building. I did not see any renovations in the room that I was shown, and I got a bit suspicious.

I paid the deposit plus rent and we moved in the following day. Auntie drove me to a place to buy a bed and a few dishes and groceries. As there was nobody else in the neighborhood, it was scary, especially at night. I could hear people passing by. I learnt later that the place was deserted because it was a high crime area and anybody who operated business there was robbed. Auntie had a real good plan for me. This house I rented had a shop at the front. We were only using one room, which we used as a kitchen, living room, and bedroom. After two days, she said that since I was going to be very bored during the day, she wanted to take me to the market so I could buy tomatoes and vegetables and sell them for her! Oh yes, she had to make use of me. I was paying the rent, I did not have any idea how long I was going to be there, and this person who was supposed to help me wanted to misuse me. I refused. I eventually found another house in a safe area near a school for Bryan.

All that time none of my family members knew where the children and I were but Anne had assured them we were safe. I went to a cyber café and sent an email to my brother Ndaba and told him we were safe and in Uganda. I had five different email addresses using different names. This was because JB was capable of hacking into my emails, which were registered in my name, anytime. My brothers helped me pay for Bryan's school fees and to buy his school supplies. I asked them to send money using the name of the lady who helped us to get a house. By the time the money got through to her, we suffered much. I would call to ask if she has received our money but she would say she had our money but was too busy to bring it over to us. Sometimes the police were going around to homes looking for illegal aliens. I was one of them since we were living there illegally. Bryan was being taught Luganda as a subject and that was a great help. He taught me in the evening. At least I knew how to ask for the prices and money in Luganda. Life was very difficult in Kampala with lots of malaria; sometimes we did not have money to go to the hospital or even to buy a meal. I am so thankful to my brothers Ndaba and Tom who throughout the time we were in Kampala would send money. The Women's Rights Advisory Program sometimes sent money. I used to go to the shop and request food on credit. I made sure I maintained good credit.

In the meantime, JB continued to terrorize people in Kenya. I had not given any instructions to any lawyer to act for me. His assumption was that Federation of Women Lawyers Kenya was my lawyer since they and the children's department helped me when he abused Bryan in 1998. In a letter he addressed to one of the lawyers he requested her to help him solve our case amicably as he did not wish the issue to be complicated. He also enclosed the following letter for them to give to me. It partly read:

To my dear wife, I, your despised and dejected but loving husband would like to state some facts to you and may be you will see some light at the end of the tunnel. Pauline, since the first day I first met you, I have lived for you and later for you and our children. I will do whatever is within my power and ability and utilize all the necessary resources to have you back to me. I have gone through a realization and confirmation by talking to my parents and noted where my mistakes are. I am not going to mention it least you interpret it wrongly that I am unfairly trying to lure you back. Pauline my dear, please come home. I miss you, I love you, you will never have a better place than with me. Please Pauline my dear come back home.

Please note that, and I repeat that I am going to do all that is within my ability, power and prowess to see that you are back to me and bet a million shillings!

Pauline, do you know you are great? Sincerely you are. You have made me the man I am now and you deserve better than this.

Your loving husband

JB

That single-spaced letter was typed and six pages long. He said all kinds of good things about me and that he was going to be the best father to the children and the best husband to me. Since he realized his previous tactics of force or threats would not work this time, he would try to sweet talk me. I did not fall for his trick.

In March 2002, I sent a letter to the Federation of Women Lawyers asking them to file a separation and to seek custody of the children for me. It took a long time because they had to send documents by email, which I printed, signed and returned by post so they could file them in court. By April 2002, JB had wrecked havoc on everybody. My lawyers and the women's rights organizations, my parents, and my brothers were not spared. They called a press conference, hoping that when the story was brought forward, JB would stop harassing them. The press conference was at the Stanley Hotel in Nairobi. The main television stations, radios, and daily newspapers attended. He had accused the director of women's rights advisory program of abducting the children and that she was demanding Kenya Shilling half a million from him! The problem with JB was that he could tell straight white lies. They organized a teleconference so I could talk to the media and make it clear that I walked out on my own free will. JB denied hurting either the children or me and that I was mentally sick. He said he was looking for me desperately so I could be treated. When he was asked if he had documentation to prove my metal health, he said he had never sought any medical treatment for me.

The following was printed in a local daily:

THE PEOPLE Daily—Nairobi April 5, 2002
Battered Wife, Two Sons Go into Hiding

A mother has gone into hiding with her two sons after 10 years of alleged humiliating torture by her husband who has been reluctant to let her go and is allegedly threatening to kill her.

Pauline Njeri Ngure, 33, walked out on her husband JB for the seventeenth time on January 9 to seek refuge from the Women's Rights Awareness Program (WRAP). She stayed there for four days before going into hiding for fear that her husband who was harassing the WRAP director would go after her.

However, her going into hiding has left WRAP and her family under siege. JB a finance administrator with Women Enterprise Development (WEDCO) which is a CARE International Program allegedly reported to Kilimani police station that WRAP had abducted his wife and two children and are holding them against their will. He has allegedly been harassing her parents.

Speaking at a press conference at The Stanley Hotel yesterday, WRAP Chairperson Anne Ngugi, however denied that the non-governmental organization had kidnapped Njeri.

Njeri was able to speak to members of the press by telephone. She confirmed that she had voluntarily opted out of her 10-year marriage following alleged continuous physical and mental abuse by her husband, which started only three months after their marriage in January 1992.

"I have not been kidnapped. I left out of my own free will. If JB is listening to me, let him know that I will never go back to him. All these years he has battered me, stripped me naked, forced me to go on my knees, beating me anywhere anytime and calls me all sorts of names including a prostitute, devil worshipper, thief, stupid, brainless and, above all, he says I can only give birth to boys. He even threw hot meat at me one time."

She said that her husband takes women to their house and sleeps with them while she sleeps with the house help, and tells his girlfriends to insult her, beats up the children including the nine-month old baby.

Several of her attempts to run away from her estranged husband have been in vain. He forcibly makes her go back. He even assaulted her elderly parents on one such occasion when she had sought refuge at her home in Limuru.

Njeri is a professional legal secretary. Her parents said yesterday they wanted the marriage to be terminated. Her mother, who could not hold back her tears throughout the press conference, pleaded with the government to come to her daughter's rescue. *"This man is very arrogant and boasts that he has a lot of money and he can do anything. We have reported to the police and they are doing nothing. Actually they are supporting him. If anything happens to my daughter, the government is to blame."*

They were accompanied by Njeri's two brothers, Ndaba wa Ngure and Tom Ngure. Speaking on behalf of the family, Tom said it would be an understatement *to say that Njeri's marriage had been hell. He took issue with the government accusing it of ignoring women's rights. He claimed that Kilimani police station where the case had been reported, have 'dropped the case as a family affair'.*

What is baffling Njeri is why the police officers have done nothing about the case. "Why have they allowed themselves to be used? Am I a criminal? I am a citizen entitled to protection. I can't remain in hiding just because of a failed marriage."

After the media highlighted my story, a female Member of Parliament called the media, which resulted in the following:

Beth Mugo has criticized the Kenyan police for "laxity, arrogance and insensitiveness in handling cases of domestic violence."

Mugo wondered why police had treated violence meted on Njeri as a 'family affair' and not a violation of fundamental human rights. She said that Njeri's plight was an example of the many women who have continued to suffer in silence due to spousal abuse. She also questioned the administration of justice and said that it had been occasioned by the fact that Njeri is a poor woman who cannot afford to 'buy justice' in a country that has become completely leprous with corruption.

Beth Mugo,
Dagoretti Member of Parliament and Assistant
Minister of Education, Kenya

After that press conference JB got more steam to harass everybody. He does not believe in defeat—fighting seems to be his cup of tea. My family wrote to the commissioner of police requesting protection for them and for me.

We the Ngure family wish to request for protection from your respected office against the harassment being meted to us and our daughter Njeri by her estranged husband JB. During the ten years that Njeri has been married to JB she has never known any stability in her home. Instead Njeri has had to endure unspeakable torture and humiliation at the hands of her ill tempered and very violent man. On each occasion that Njeri has tried to leave her abusive husband, he abducts her back, beats her up and threatens to kill her when she runs away again. JB appears to enjoy a very good rapport and influence with the police.

Njeri has suffered in the hands of Kilimani police, Kasarani police, Pangani police, Buruburu police and Kiusmu police. Instead of protecting her, these police station gang up with Njeri's husband to harass her and make her go back to him. The Women's Rights Advisory Program director has severally been taken to Kilimani police station but luckily unlike Njeri they are always released after being made to record statements. Our parents had been summoned to the same police station by the DCIO where they were forced to record a statement about Njeri.

How come that the man who beats up his wife and children and her parents too and even has her locked up in police cells appear to the police to be the wronged party and hence the victim?

The women's rights organization wrote the same request to the police commissioner but my rich husband continued to enjoy police support.

Fortunately, from the day my story appeared in the media my parents and women's organizations received a lot of support from organizations and individuals in Kenya. The program of CARE International, at which JB was a financial manager, terminated his contract. This made him go mad completely. He sent me an email and told me that since I had left my work and run away, and had made him get fired, we were at par and so I could stay with the children and I should never think he would ever help me bring them up. The fight continued but JB was not the man to give up until he laid his hands on me.

Letter, 18 April 2002 from JB:

> *Dear Pauline,*
>
> *I would like to state that I am out of your life and I need to send elders to your parents to end this marriage once and for all. Please call me through my cell phone so that we can agree on a date. I have no reservations at all and positively answer your prayer to me through the press. Your quick response will be highly appreciated.*
>
> *By a copy of this letter to FIDA and WRAP, please note that I appreciate your belated action to take this matter to court. By the way, did you ever wonder why I declined to use any other statute for this marriage? I*

*think you have the answers now. I will never love you
again, I bet a million dollars!*

This is the same man who bet a million shillings a
few months to love me for ever and never let me go. This
time the bet was in dollars and not shillings.

I used to cry, especially when my children got sick.
There was a time when both boys were down with malaria
and they had high fevers. I removed their clothes, put
them on the bed, and mopped them with a wet cloth to
reduce the fever. I did not have money to take them to the
doctor. When I realized their condition had deteriorated,
I asked a doctor to treat them on credit. He hesitated but
I assured him that I would pay him as soon as I received
money from home.

First Steps to Canada

Amazingly, Bryan was doing very well in school. The lowest mark he got was a 70 percent and that was in Luganda, a new language to him. This was so unlike when we were home, where he was getting zeros in almost all subjects because of stress. Ours was a two-room house; we used paraffin stove or a charcoal stove to cook. We had to buy water from a lady called Carol. She had a tap where she used to sell water from. It was one block from our house. Water was sold in 20-liter containers; sometimes when I was sick, Bryan bought water and carried it home. He was such a wonderful help. Sometimes I asked him if he wanted us to go back home since there were many problems in Uganda. He would cry and beg me not to ever take him back to JB's house.

Corruption in Africa is the order of the day. We used to live in the same compound with the landlady. She never paid for electricity as she had disconnected the meter with the help of some unscrupulous people who worked for the electric company. If she was caught in a spot check, our electricity was disconnected for as long as three weeks. If we used candles, which were very expensive, it was difficult for Bryan to do homework. But it did not hinder him from doing well in school.

After a long time I contacted my Auntie; she was very happy to hear from me. She came to see us and I explained the circumstances that made us move from the house she found for us. Since my cell phone was usually down because of low battery charge—most of the time we did not have electricity—email was the only way to communicate with people at home. I carried Kevin on my back in the hot Kampala weather, went to a cyber café to check for and send emails, and then rushed home before Bryan returned from school.

One evening Auntie called and told me she had talked to a friend named Stella who worked as a counsellor. Auntie wanted Stella to see me. When they came they found both children very sick. Auntie had already told Stella all she knew about me. Some people just wanted to see me because they thought whatever I said could never happen to any human being. When Stella saw all our problems, she gave me some reading material and promised to return the following Saturday. That was the last time I saw her! Any person I made contact with, I made sure I told them of the consequences they might suffer if JB found they were helping me.

I later talked to her when I came to Canada and she told me that she had decided to pass my case to someone else. Stella's one and only visit is the reason we got help to come to Canada. The following week Auntie called and told me she would drive us to meet a lady who would try to help us get asylum. She had started receiving threatening calls from JB. Through his efforts, together with the Kenya police, Kenya Posts and Telecommunications, and Kencell Communications, he had tracked Auntie's number because the Women's Rights Advisory Program used to call her and of course, all of Anne's telephones were tapped! Auntie was a lawyer in the Ugandan government. She used to be chauffeured in a 4 X 4 Trooper. One evening when she was being driven home, she received a mysterious call from JB who said he was my brother and wanted to talk to me urgently. All along I had warned her that if she ever received a call from anybody asking to speak with me, she should automatically know that it was JB. She pretended she was an old woman who did not understand a word of English. She started making noises in Luganda. This really annoyed JB; he hung up, never to call her again. It was a Friday evening. Auntie froze. She called to tell me how bad things were, and I told her not to worry, as all along I knew that one day JB would call her. When I look back at such situations, it looks like a movie.

On appointment day, Auntie came with her driver to pick us up. We talked to a very kind American lady. She was the head of the program and her work was only to recommend the case to the protection manager, who in turn would listen to the person seeking asylum and pass on his recommendation to the resettlement manager. Lilly booked me to see the protection manager the following Monday. This was late November 2002. Unfortunately I lost the small notebook, which I used to write all the important dates. I was surprised by the way that man was holding a senior position and he was not serious. During the interview, he kept receiving phone calls from friends and when he came back to talk to me he would ask me, "Where were we?" It was discouraging and at the end of the interview, he said, "I hear what you are saying but I don't think we can help you. You do not have enough documentary evidence to show that your husband is a threat or that your life is in danger." I thanked him for his time and I left. At the reception there was a very kind lady called Mary. She escorted me and asked how the interview went. When I told her, she told me that she would try to pass my file to the senior protection manager. After a week I was asked to visit the senior protection manager. By that time, I knew how to reach there by public means and did not need to tell Auntie. She was becoming a pain because once she was sent my documents and refused to give them to me, saying they were only safe with her. She was also calling that office, asking them about my case. According to policy, they would not discuss cases with third parties.

My appointment was with Steve at 10 a.m.; he listened patiently, sympathized, and said he would do all he could to get us out of Uganda as quickly as possible. He told me after reading my documents; he had come to the conclusion that our lives were in danger. Some of the required documents were still with Auntie. The office said if I could get the documents faxed from my home, they would still work. I called Tom in Kenya but he was not reachable. I tried Ndaba and he was not reachable. I tried Ndaba's wife Njeri; she was not reachable either. I did not give up. I called Anne and asked her to get Tom to fax the documents. Within half an hour, all the documents were in Uganda. My awesome brother Tom! Even today, if I need any documents, Tom always makes it happen.

Steve postponed all his other appointments until he had finished my case. He had to type a report and his recommendations to the resettlement officer. He asked me not to go home because he had booked an appointment for me to see the resettlement officer that afternoon. I had left the boys on their own but with enough food.

Bryan was old enough to look after Kevin; to feed him, and change his diapers.

Nelson was from the Netherlands. He asked me to give him a few minutes as he was still reading my documents. I waited for twenty long minutes. The first question he asked was, "Are you ok? Do you need water or anything to drink?" He told me he was there to help me and not to laugh or make fun of me. He told me since he had read my documents, he would not ask me any questions because he did not think there was anything more he needed to know. He picked up the phone and called his secretary, and asked her to tell everyone working on my case to stay that evening until my case was done. He said he was going to write a report to the Canadian Consulate in Kampala and that my file was to be taken there the following morning. He told me if the Canadian government was not ready to help immediately, he would try another country. He asked if we had food at home and if the children were ok and I told him we were fine. He asked if I had money for airtime on my cell phone; he asked me to make sure I kept it fully charged and that I should call him in case of anything. He gave me a direct number, his cell phone, and his home number. The following morning, he called to say he had sent my file as promised and was trying to make an appointment for me as soon as possible. He also told me he would try to get us out of where we lived and take us to a safe place.

I could not believe what was happening and so fast. Yes, it is true God is alive and He never leaves those who trust and believe in Him. The following day Mary asked us to get ready, as they wanted to relocate us. We had very few things to pack—just a few clothes. When they finally came, we were ready. We locked the house and informed the landlady we were going to Auntie's for a few days. The safe place was *so* safe we could not get out on our own unless they came for us. Steve continued to call to check on how we were doing. By now, I had lost contact with my family and they were very worried. After Tom sent that fax, I was instructed not to communicate with anybody apart from the people who were helping me.

When we were taken to the Canadian Consulate in Kampala I met a very good person who also said he was not going to put me through questions because he already had read my file. He promised to fly us to Canada in a week. Was I dreaming? He said we needed a medical test and would request that the appointments be set up as soon as possible. That time fear gripped me. I was going to be tested for HIV AIDS! JB had been sleeping around and infecting me with sexually transmitted diseases. How sure was I that I did not have the HIV virus? That thought almost made me go crazy. If you are infected, you cannot get asylum. It was time to call upon God.

A man at the consulate greeted me in my language. He made me a cup of nice Kenyan tea. He was a born Canadian but said that he had lived in my hometown for twenty years while working at the Bata shoe factory. I still remember seeing that old man seeing us off. He escorted us to the vehicle, held my hand, looked at my boys and told me, "You are a very brave and strong woman. Hang in there and at the end of this journey, you will live a happy life together with your children forever." We were taken back to the safe place.

On Monday, December 02, 2002, a driver took us for our medicals. We were not supposed to wait in the reception area for fear of being seen by somebody who might know us, so we were taken for the medicals immediately. The driver said he was rushing somewhere for an errand and would come back before we were done, but we finished before he returned and had to wait outside, as the reception area was full. Outside, a man pretended to read a newspaper when I looked his way; when I turned away, he looked at me. I got frightened because my driver had not arrived, so we went back into the clinic. The receptionist was surprised to see us, but I told her I needed to call the office urgently. She dialled and asked them to come for us immediately, as things were not looking good. As she was still talking, the driver arrived and we dashed out. When that newspaper-reading man saw us getting into the vehicle, he dashed as if to follow us, removed his cell phone, dialled a number, and started talking. We could not go directly to the office or even home. I don't know Kampala very well, so I have no clue where we drove. I was shaken and so were my children. Fear is bad. I would never wish it on anybody, having to go through that kind of trauma.

The following day, the driver came to tell me to disable my cell phone because Steve had received a mysterious phone call. He was the senior protection manager who used to call me frequently to update me. Things were going from bad to worse. They said if they needed to communicate with me, they would call the owner of our house.

In all the days and months I was in Uganda, that was my longest and last week there. No communication, no going out. I spent my time in the bedroom with my boys praying and reading the Bible. All along I trusted in the Lord that the medical results would not stop us.

Early in December 2002, a vehicle with Canadian consulate plates came to the compound. We were still in the bedroom. Mary came to the bedroom and told us we were required to sign a document as we might be leaving early in the week. We signed!

The weekend was long and tiring. Mary came to see us on Sunday afternoon. She knew we were leaving but did not tell me for sure. The strange thing was that people were so much afraid that nobody trusted the other to an extent of not even trusting me. On Monday morning, I woke up early, prepared breakfast, and as we were eating, something impressed me to tell the children to eat quickly as we were leaving soon. In mid-morning, I received a telephone call. It was Mary saying, "Get yourself and the boys ready. We are picking you up at 3 and your flight is at 7 tonight!" It was too good to be true. The only words that came from my mouth were; "Thank you! God is faithful."

I hung up. I went to the bedroom and cried. It is true that God did not create my children and me to suffer for the rest of our lives. God heard and answered our prayers. It was the end of a battle, a battle bravely fought and won by us with God's help!

Just before 3 in the afternoon, a big truck arrived and we were ready to go. I told my children we could not leave without going back into the bedroom, just the three of us, and say, "Thank You God for saving us. Thank you for answering our prayers."

Other passengers have to check in two hours before departure time; in our case, it was just before the plane's doors shut. No hanging around at the airport for us! People at the office insisted on seeing us before we left, so we were driven to the office, said our good-byes to those who worked around the clock to help us. Some cried as they hugged us. I cried too. They said they loved us so much that they wanted us to leave that country as quickly as possible so we would be safe.

As we were going to board the plane, a Kenya Airways plane landed from Nairobi. I froze: JB could be on that plane. He might have tapped the telephones. The worst could happen if he was a passenger on that plane and saw us boarding. That was when my legs failed me. I could not move. I had the baggage in one hand and Kevin on the other. Bryan was beside me. I was wearing my veil and Bryan's cap covered part of his face. Bryan started crying, pleading to leave with me to walk. All over sudden, I asked myself "What am I doing? I have fought all this battle just to fail my children and I at the last minute?" I held Bryan with my left hand and walked toward the airplane, climbed the stairs, and found our seats.

We only had air tickets to Ethiopia, a two-hours flight from Uganda. At the Addis Ababa airport someone was waiting for us with travel documents and tickets to Canada. They did not do that in Uganda for fear of JB tracing us before we boarded. The journey was long and tiring; I never had such a long flight in my life. But best of all, I knew we were going to Canada. I had no idea where in Canada or how I was going to live. How I was to start my new life was all I thought about in the plane. What kind of people I would meet? How would I cope?

As of this writing, 2005, Kevin just turned four and Bryan will soon be ten. They are happy and I am happy too. I will forever remain grateful to everyone who listened to me, believed me and suffered because of us. The government of Canada is wonderful. They respect human rights and recognize women are human beings and not just women.

JB continued to harass me by email. In November 2003, he sent me this email

Hi. How have you been for the last two years or so? I would appreciate if you take what I put here very seriously and put jokes and innuendos aside. I would also beg you to be just a bit humane and this will avoid a lot of hassles either in your or my life. I have tried to extend an olive branch to you for the sake of our lives and those of our sons but to no avail. Now, back to why I write this mail. I am ready to use all my money to get you back to me. I reiterate here that I am not negotiating with you but you must do as I say!

You have tried your best to make me poor and irrelevant but I don't think you have control of this. So the big question is whether you are ready to co-operate or not. If you don't reply to this mail, I will assume automatically that you don't want to and I will take charge.

JB

I never said a word to him. I never replied and I never will. Because of such threats, when my father died in February 2005, I could not go home. JB hoped I would; he had people at the airport waiting for me and others dispatched around my home area. When he did not find me, he got so angry he sent this email:

Hi. Sorry for losing your father, an icon you cherished. Sorry that you could not be there in person to pay your last respects. Pass my regards to my sons and make sure to inform them that their troubles on earth are now less! "She who wishes daughter whores gets punishment and long life, burying sons, daughters and husbands." May God forgive me for passing judgement.

Your husband, JB

Since I left him, I had never cried because of his abuse. That day I cried and blocked his email. I am sure he continues to send many more but they will never reach me. If I were still living with him, he sure would have said the same words to me. I do not know why he hated my parents and my family so much.

There are so many women going through what I went through. What will they do? Sit and wait to die? Why can't the Kenya government treat women like human beings? As always said, women's rights are human rights. Let everybody practice this. The slogan of the Women's Rights Advisory Program is good: "Real men do not hit women."

If you are a real man, please do not do it. If you hit women and children, you are not a real man. Which side do you want to be on? I suffered so much at the hands of a man, but I have nothing against men. I am a mother of two great boys and want to bring them up so they will respect, love, and treat women the way they would like their mother to be treated. My father was a great man (God rest his soul in eternal peace) who my mother says never hit her.

As a survivor of domestic violence I would like other women who are still suffering to know there is hope out there. There is one person if not two who can listen, understand, and help. If your husband is a wife batterer, he will never change. Do not think of revenge because it does not pay, the best thing is to leave. If he is a threat to your life and that of your children, read this book for your tips on survival tactics and eventually you will be free.

We arrived in Toronto in mid-December 2002. I was shocked when the lady at the counter just by looking at me decided that I was not able to communicate in English. Probably in her working life at the airport she only met refugees who did not speak English. I stood in front of her for about three minutes. I did not know why she was not talking to me until when she told one of her colleagues, "I have a very complicated case here. This lady is from Kenya and we do not have any interpreter." I smiled and told her, "Maybe we can use sign language."

Survival Skills—Two Views

I conclude my story with two stories: adjusting to a new country and some concrete suggestions if you are in an abusive relationship.

Winter in Canada

I had only read about those cold Canadian winters but never thought I would experience one. The people who welcomed us knew exactly what we faced: they gave us winter coats, snow boots, mittens, and toques. On our trip in from the airport, I noticed the van clock said it was 5 p.m. but outside it was dark already. Dark? At this hour? Of course, I thought, the clock was not working properly, but when I asked, the driver he said it was indeed 5 p.m.

"But it's fully dark," I exclaimed. What followed was my first lesson in the realities of a Canadian winter: short days, and long, long nights. A few other things were new to us.

After a night in a hotel, we flew from Toronto to far-distant Saskatchewan, landing in Regina where three people waited-the pastor of a church that had co-sponsored us with the government; a government representative, and David, an African man. My only link to them was the plastic bag we were given in Kampala-our identification badge. Picture us getting off the plane in Regina-me with all our hand luggage in one hand and little Kevin in the other. Bryan had the identification badge. Our welcomers saw us immediately and introduced themselves. I knew we had reached our destination, but I was *so* nervous. I did not know what to expect. Where were we being taken? I soon found out we were to drive for an hour to Moose Jaw where we were taken to a hotel room that had a small kitchen, two beds and a dining area. The friendly lady who bought milk, bread, butter, and some fruit told me she worked across the street at a multicultural center and would pick us up in the morning so I could be tested for my English language skills.

"What's this all about?" I wondered. "I have spoken English all my life and now they want to put me in an English class?" An elderly lady conducted the test and concluded I was to be put in the highest level to learn English. "This must be another type of English," I thought. Not so. I was placed in a class where the students could not even construct a proper sentence.

After a few days we were moved into a government house. Bryan went to school and was also placed in an English as second language class. By now he was seven so he went into grade two. When I collected his first report card, his teacher wanted to accelerate him to the next grade because she realized he was not being challenged enough in her class. I politely refused, as I wanted him in a grade suitable to his age.

Moose Jaw is a city of 35,000 people, but was too small for me. I could not figure out what to do. After my first job interview, I was told I could start the following day. I had to leave Kevin with neighbors and soon knew such an arrangement could not last. I knew nothing about subsidies or day cares, so I had to quit. When I told someone at a multicultural center I wanted to re-locate to a bigger city, I was told that if I did, I would lose my government assistance. That didn't sound correct, so I called immigration; they said I was in a free country and I could re-locate as I wished. All I had to do was report to the immigration office to continue receiving assistance.

Thanks to the help of a lovely Moose Jaw lady named Louise who cared for the boys while I was gone, I made a fast trip to Calgary. Maybe my desire to go there raised a few eyebrows, but I had come such a great distance and had moved so many times, a twenty-hour round trip drive was nothing to me.

I travelled overnight, found a house the next day, and travelled back to Moose Jaw that night.

We moved to Calgary in July 2003; I found a temporary part-time job, learned about day-care and how to apply for a subsidy. In less than a month, I had a permanent full-time job.

Even with a job, it was not going to be easy. I needed a reliable vehicle. Problem. Car dealerships wanted a credit history before offering financing. I had no credit history. Talk about frustrating! How could I get a credit history without being given a credit? Finally, my friend Anita took me to a dealership and they said if I could get a letter from a bank in Kenya it would help. I told them I was not getting *any* letters from Kenya; the only letter they would get from me was from my employer. Surprisingly, they called my boss to confirm that I worked there; he faxed a letter and the following day my application was approved. That was one problem, a big one, solved.

I applied for a credit card and got the same story. My employer tried to talk to them but they said I had no credit history. It took a while to convince them I had a job, but I finally got a credit card.

I had had ten years' driving experience in Kenya but was told it did not count. When I tried to insure my vehicle, my premium was very high because I did not have North American driving experience. I soon learnt that Canadian drivers are very responsible and generally keep to the speed limit. I quickly got accustomed to 50 kilometers per hour—no wonder they said I needed North American driving experience! When I got my first speeding ticket, I learnt my lesson and never went beyond the speed limit again.

I had never heard of jay walking. In Kenya we cross the road anywhere, any time—even on the busiest highways. All we do is look both ways and if it's safe, we cross, whether the lights are red or green. This is what

I did in Canada, until someone told me I could get a ticket for jay walking. What? A hundred dollar fine? I changed.

In my new country, a woman is treated like a human being. The law protects children. I couldn't be in a better country. Canada has given me back and guaranteed my dignity and the freedom to laugh and enjoy life again! Men, even if they do not know you, open and hold doors for women. They let women in and out of elevators first. How *nice* to be in such a country! I hope one day the Kenya government will wake up and recognize women and children as human beings. I do not know what kind of gospel they need to hear or who can preach it to them. They need to hear that women's rights are human rights.

If you are in an abusive relationship

I know how you think. I have been there. You think you cannot escape the relationship. You think things will change for the better. You think you need him. You tell yourself you do not have the financial ability to be on your own. You have convinced yourself there is no escape. The abuse has gone beyond bruises and tears; now he controls your actions and how you think. You are the total victim. I was once in your shoes.

When I left, I escaped with nothing. In the course of my struggle in Uganda, there was a time I almost walked barefooted. I had no money for something as simple as shoes: my only pair were torn, but that did not change my heart to look back. If anything, it encouraged me to push ahead!

Like you, I was afraid of questions like "Where will I go?" "Where will I take my children?" "Who will help us?"

Make the move! You cannot believe how things will happen in your favor.

- As a survivor of domestic violence I know there *is* hope out there. All you need is one person, perhaps two, who will listen, understand, and help.
- If your husband is a wife batterer, he will never change. I know this from sad experience.
- Do not think of revenge. It does not pay and you could end up suffering more. Leave.
- If he is a threat to your life and that of your children, do not wait for him to chop off your legs or gouge out your eyes as we have witnessed in Kenya. Leave. Perhaps something that extreme does not happen in North America and if it does, at least those who does it faces the full force of the law unlike in Kenya where we practice the rule of the jungle. It doesn't matter; even one bruise is one bruise too many. Leave.
- Do not stay because you think your children must have a father. What's better? An abusive father or no father at all? What's better? A physically or emotionally scarred mother or a mom who happens to be single? Many single women have brought up responsible children, children who respect their mothers, children who would not allow anyone to hurt their mother, children who would never hurt a woman. But if you bring them up in a home where they always see their father beating their mother, they are being trained to become wife batterers and child abusers. Protect your children and your children's

children. Save your little ones from an abusive home. Leave.

Many women's organizations all over the world cater to the needs of domestic violence victims. Call them. They are in the phone book. Do not fear, they are there to help you, to listen, and find not only temporary help but also permanent solutions to your problems.

Tips

- Talk to a trusted friend or relative who knows about your abusive relationship. Ask them to help you with money if you do not have any. If you can't trust anybody, then trust the women's rights organizations. Tell them the truth about your situation, about your lack of money, about your fear, about the level of abuse. They will not be shocked and they will understand. You are not the first one they have helped to escape from the hell of an abusive relationship. They will take you to a safe place.
- Do NOT leave your children behind – they will be mistreated and you will never have the peace you are looking for.
- Do not use your home telephone or your cell phone. He will trace your calls and know what you are planning. My abusive husband did. Use a pay phone and be safe.
- Do not contact anybody, including family members.
- Keep your escape plans to yourself and your lawyer. It sounds awful to say

- "Do not trust anyone," but that is the truth of the matter. Your life and that of your children can be at risk.
- Give the women's organization a number of a trusted family member to call so they can be told when you are safe.
- If you have a cell phone, turn it off. Do not check for messages. He will leave tons of messages, promising never to hurt you again. Do not open letters from him. If he comes to the door, do not open it. Weeping, he will tell you he loves you.
- Do not be tempted to try again. Do not be swayed by his entreaties, by his tears, by his loving promises. He will not change. He cannot change because he is lying to you. Remember he has lied before.
- Seek legal advice. Since most of the women's rights lawyers are free, you are guaranteed legal representation without financial worries.
- Tell them you want legal custody of the children.
- Get restraining orders.
- Know how to contact the police and don't hesitate to report to them. But if you are in Kenya, do not dare go near a police station, they will lock you up and call your husband. Stay as far as possible from Kenya police especially Kilimani Police Station.
- If you have property, the lawyer needs to know you want your fair share. Have your documents well in order before you make your break.

- If you know that claims to money or property will threaten you or the children, tell your lawyer.
- If you know that even with a restraining order, your husband is still a threat, tell your lawyer and ask for advice.
- Your lawyer can only act on your instructions, so if you keep changing things, they will lose interest in helping. Be consistent, be firm, and be strong especially
- for your children. If you have left, stay away and be strong in your determination to make a new life, a safer life.
- The children need to be in school but if hiding, moving, fleeing, or being safe means losing a semester or a year of their school life, they will be supportive.
- If you believe in God, put your trust and hope in Jesus and you will be happy at the end of the journey.

Do not feel ashamed of yourself because of the inhuman action inflicted on you by your husband or male partner. *He* is the one who should be ashamed, not you! He is the guilty one, not you. People will not hate you or laugh at you because you have been abused. They will respect you for having the courage to leave.

Until I was given asylum by the Canadian government, I did not know that one could be a refugee because of a domestic situation. Ask your lawyer to guide you on how to seek asylum. In most cases, you will only be granted asylum if you cross a border. Ask for directions to the

United Nations High Commission for Refugees. They are kind, helpful, and listen to everybody.

- Have documents to support your case. The most important documents are court documents. Your lawyer can identify which ones are the most useful.
- Do not be intimidated.
- Do not panic.
- Do not keep changing your story. Stick to the truth and keep sane. Your children need you now, more than at any other time. Be strong for them and be strong for yourself.
- Do not tell everybody your problems; they will not or cannot help. Make your lawyer your best friend and when the time comes, you will get out of the mess without anybody knowing.

About the Author

A legal assistant, Pauline Ngure was born and raised in Kenya. Now the mother of two boys, Pauline endured ten years of humiliating torture from a violently abusive husband and the complicit Kenya police. She was given asylum by the Canadian government after the Kenya government would not protect her and her children from her husband.

Finding faith, hope, and strength in her God, women rights organizations and her family who risked their own safety to ensure hers, she fled Kenya to a neighboring country where she sought and found not only a refuge in Canada, but also a whole new future for herself and the boys.

An ugly story with a beautiful ending, this story will not only inspire, but also instruct the reader as to what can and should be done in the face of spousal abuse and government disinterest.